Reasonably Gay

Reasonably Gay

2013 - 2014

Chad Felix Greene

Independently published

Contents

Introduction

In 2013, I decided I wanted to become a political writer. I'd been active on political Twitter for a while, built a bit of an audience and felt like I had an interesting perspective to share with the world. I started my first website, *Reasonably Gay*. My writings reflected the style of debate and argument I engaged in, mostly in Facebook comments and long Twitter threads. I had very strong opinions on just about everything.

Although I felt driven to advocate for a wide variety of conservative arguments, on social media it was my perspective as a member of the LGBT community that got the most engagement and reaction. Sure, my position on the minimum wage or abortion earned likes during arguments with angry liberals, but it was my arguments about contemporary LGBT issues that really captured the attention of my followers.

I wasn't the first and certainly not the only gay conservative voice out there, Bruce Carroll, better known as GayPatriot, waved that flag long before I entered the conversation. But for some reason, my arguments stood out and I began to get noticed by bigger conservative personalities.

A few months after I began blogging and receiving positive feedback, I took a risk and sent a submission titled, *Gay Rights: An Unnecessary Battle*, to one of my favorite conservative websites at the time, *American Thinker*. The editor responded more quickly than I expected with a simple, *'Thank you for writing this,'* and an offer to publish it on the site. It was my first published article and I felt a surge of validation and accomplishment. I shared it absolutely everywhere and with everyone.

The article gained a lot of attention and so I submitted another controversial argument challenging the LGBT position at the time. Throughout 2014 I would be published many times on *American Thinker* and the experience dramatically shaped my writing for the next decade. I experienced the editing process, rejection, controversy and possibly the most unnerving aspect of article-writing, the comments section.

The confidence I gained from this experience launched my career as a writer and helped build my reputation as an unconventional conservative voice unafraid to challenge the established narrative. I continued writing on my blog as well, building a catalogue of arguments, some strong, others needing development. I found my voice as a writer.

This collection is made up of many of my writings during this time period, both published and unpublished. As a time capsule, these writings open a window into the controversial topics of the day and what I and many others in the conservative movement deeply cared about.

They bring us back to when the LGBT movement was on the brink of both winning their fight for marriage and losing the gains in public support they'd won a decade earlier. We remember feminism before the gender identity movement shattered it into factions and how so many of their insane arguments defined conservative conversation. We see a conservative movement on the edge of losing much of the culture war, but simultaneously preparing for a revolution in rightwing speech and political influence.

For me, though, these writings remind me of what I cared about when I was working two jobs, hopelessly dating, balancing friendships with political activism and deciding my place in the world. While many of my views have evolved or changed completely since then, its enjoyable to see who I was in this window of time and what I felt was important enough to put to paper and share with the world.

Living the Dream

November 10th, 2013

I WAS RECENTLY ASKED about what my "dream" was and if I could instantly have it, what would I do? To be honest I have absolutely no way to answer that. In our current social model this means I am not very insightful or focused on the future and I shouldn't be taken seriously. I don't have a dream. The closest thing I can come up with is an ideal outcome without a specific path to get there. I want to have enough money to not be in debt, own a house and take care of my personal utility use without concern. I want to be able to immediately assist friends with financial needs. I want to feel safe when I come home. I want to not worry if my cat Freddie decides to pee on the floor. That is my "dream."

I owe more in student loans than I make in two years and have made stupid choices that crashed my credit rating and keep me in a perpetual paycheck to paycheck survival mode trying to catch up. My college degrees are theoretically positive things I can maybe use in the future, but I am currently not in a career path that uses them or even requires them. I don't have enough experience to move ahead anyways.

I am stuck in what is likely a familiar situation that most of my generation understands. My generation has fringe success stories and girls who married men of the previous generation who knew what the hell they were doing. The rest of us are either still in college working towards a degree with absolutely no career path in mind or are slowly working our way through 2nd level job positions and watching most of our money disappear into the endless hole called Debt.

Why is this happening? I had access to the best education, healthcare, food and personal development of any generation who has ever lived on this planet. I grew up in the 80's and 90's before computers were popular but after liberal "find yourself" classes were in full swing. From age 4 to 17 I had 9 months of each year to learn every intellectual skill I could. Even living in a low-income family, I never starved or had to worry about my water supply or where to use the bathroom. There is absolutely no reason for me, or anyone of my generation, to be in the situation we are in today.

My grandparents were on their own as teenagers in a world with absolutely no government assistance programs, no credit programs, no credit cards, no student loans, barely any formal education and a complete and utter "you're on your own kid" attitude from all of society. My grandmother lived in a shack wallpapered with newspaper and no running water or indoor toilet. She went to school – on foot – for most of her childhood in a one-room schoolhouse that taught 1st through 8th grade by one teacher. She graduated high school at 15 and left home to go work. She worked several lower-class jobs until she got married to my grandfather and then in her 30's restarted as the first woman realtor in our area.

My grandfather went into the Navy and began working at a railroad station when he got out. He retired from that railroad station. My grandmother's 2nd husband went into the Army and began working as a truck driver when he got out. He retired as a truck driver at age 70. I barely graduated high school because I was convinced I was going to run away to California with a man I met on the internet to become a movie star. I was serious about it.

I think the difference between my grandparent's generation and mine is that they believed they had to build a life for themselves and mine is still waiting for someone else to hand it to us. My grandmother also wanted to be a movie star, but life got in the way. Today we think of this as a sad story. If she had just gone to "live her dream" and run away to California she could have made it! We love stories of people who struggled against all odds and made it big. Actors who left their homes in safe, cozy, middle-America with only a suitcase and a dream now smile in front of cameras on red carpets adored by millions. Worse, today people don't even need to pack a suitcase – they just upload a video and become instant celebrities!

Kids dream of being models, athletes and movie stars and when life gets in the way they ignore it and keep reaching for those damn stars. But isn't that the message we have been given for years now? Disney, Movies, TV Shows, Reality TV etc. has drilled into us that the only people who are ever truly happy in life are the ones who risked everything to make their dreams come true. The part of the story they don't mention is that the other hundred thousand people also trying to make their dreams come true weren't as lucky.

Listening to Kathy Griffin's book: *Official Book Club Selection: A Memoir According to Kathy Griffin* made me realize that most of the stars we see all went to the same schools and joined the same union and made it through a lot of hard work and connections. They didn't just wander into Hollywood and get their first big movie. They took acting classes and worked for years doing nightly performances to get noticed.

We Are Marshall was being filmed at my college, Marshall University, while I was attending, I got to see just some of the work put into filming a scene. I lined up to be an extra but wasn't selected and watching them be herded around (pun intended) and seeing the endless repetition of the same scene over and over made me realize that being a movie star was just not what I wanted to do. I have written five children's books and people always ask me how successful I am, and I smile when I say I have made just about $40.00 altogether. Dreams do not just happen because she you *reaaaally* wish for them to happen. Its shockingly difficult. My generation is not built for difficult work or patience. The generation after me is even less so.

One of my favorite stories about my grandmother's 2nd husband is how at 19 he got his first paycheck, and he opened a savings account. He deposited $5.00 into it and then every paycheck after he put in $5.00. Over time he put in a little more and a little more, but he never touched the account. He did not withdraw the money until he retired at 70. He literally had a life's savings. I do not have money in my account from last paycheck when I get to this paycheck.

Looking over job opportunities and looking at the LinkedIn profiles of successful people I currently know, I see a pattern of intention and purpose. The employers want specific skills and the successful people planned education to obtain those skills. Degrees in Business, Leadership and Communications seem ridiculous until you realize they can bring in good money. I went to college because I was 21 and felt like a loser. I took college classes for the hell of it. I managed to get two degrees...but not useful ones. I hear "well, I'm sure most people wish they had chosen better majors in college," far too often from equally disappointed fellow millennials.

Kids now have access to information beyond anything I could have imaged at their same age. They are learning so quickly they could easily be the most intelligent and knowledgeable generation of human beings who have ever lived. But they are also just as likely to be sitting on the couch watching Netflix, updating their Facebook pages on their phones and waiting for their food card to refill.

When people ask me why I am so grumpy at liberalism, which they often attribute to the vast access to all this knowledge, this is why. Yes, we now have government programs and loans to make sure every child can go to college. Every school has an iPad or computer for every student. Kids are fully marinated in multicultural sensitivity and endless awareness campaigns. They have been taught to be so self-aware they can barely look up from their phones long enough to see a telephone pole and not walk into it. But none of them believe they are responsible for building their own lives or wealth.

The drive that caused my grandmother to seek education to give her the necessary skills to make more money is gone. The motivation my grandmother's 2nd husband had to save money his entire life so he could be safe and retire makes no sense to people now. No one looks at college as a tool to get a better job. People see college as an entitlement.

We have all been so focused on "reaching for the stars" and "following our own bliss, whatever that may be," that we don't have the basic skills to feed and clothe ourselves. Can't you try for your dream though? Why should you suffer and toil doing something you hate for 40 years? Isn't it worth the risk?

Starting your own business, going to school at 35 for a useful degree, working full time and doing art shows on weekends – those are risks and those are ways people reach their dreams. But it is also just as effective to work and earn money so that you can focus on more dream-like endeavors later in life. We have been convinced that you must achieve your life's purpose by age 23 or it's too late for you. The truth is ugly.

My grandparent's generation was so motivated, focused and determined because they lived in a cruel and cold capitalistic world that didn't care if they starved on the streets. They had to build their own security because no one else would take care of them. My generation is cozy and comforted by the knowledge that the government will always be there if we fall, and we never have to worry about food or clothing for ourselves or our children. We have no need to fight for our own futures because it's being handled for us as we speak.

Ironically, we praise and celebrate people on shows like, *America's Next Top Model,* for giving up everything, leaving their families and children, jobs and school for that "one shot" at celebrity. We think this is brave and full of virtue. We should be praising people who focus on building their lives in tangible ways like saving money, making good credit choices, planning their education, being aggressive in their business, etc. Those people are truly risking everything and being brave. They are relying on themselves for their own success. Just like TV reality shows, though, most of us would prefer to stand before a judge panel that decides our fate than be responsible for our own successes and failures.

Morally Righteous Business

November 15th, 2013

ESSENTIALLY THE CONCEPT OF a business is simply one person offering a product or service that is intended to make another person's life more convenient in exchange for something they find valuable. That's it. All of business can be summed up into that sentence. Aside from land ownership, everything else a person needs to survive and thrive is available to them. People can grow their own food, make their own clothes and build their own houses. Everything down to the screws and needles can be created by a person who chooses to do so. We do not need businesses to provide anything for us at all.

The reason business exists in America is due to the freedom we have to build our own lives. Under other forms of government to which our ancestors fled, a person was dependent upon the good graces of the state to provide food and services to them. They could not do for themselves. In America, they could. That is the *American Dream* concept. You could come from any place in the world and build your life from the bottom up. Freedom.

Obviously, each person making everything they need or want themselves is tedious and unnecessary. If you can make great jam and can food and I can grow food, then why don't we work out an exchange together? Businesses organized trade and allowed individuals to specialize in the creation of a service or product. This spawned dozens more as each individual product required individual parts which each company specialized in and on and on. A network of these organizations flourished, and natural competition ensured balance. With a standardized money system, it fit so well together that anyone with the willingness to go out and build a unique product or service could become a millionaire.

Think of every product you own. Think of every part of that product from the container, wrapper, ink on the label etc., all of that started by individuals creating industry. Now just as not everyone can or is willing to build from scratch everything they need or want, not everyone can or is willing to build their own business. Some people choose to instead work *for* someone else.

Let's say you decide to build widgets and you find both suppliers of widget parts and a market to sell widgets and you begin your business. You decide when to open your store based on your personal life and your willingness to create opportunity to sell your widgets. If you open from 8AM to 5PM you can sell 50 widgets. But if you stay open until 7PM you could sell 75 widgets. All of this is up to you as the owner. As long as you meet the financial needs to pay your suppliers and keep a tidy profit you can open and close as you please.

This assumes you own your store. Land ownership has typically been more legal and had its share of difficulties which is for another discussion, but typically early businesses owned the land or the building for their store. Yet another business would be purchasing multiple chunks of land or stores and renting it to people who wish to use it for their own store. "Overhead" refers to the basics of keeping the business open and running. Profit is the money you have left over. Something that truly makes me scratch my head is the outrage and disgust liberals have for the intention to seek profit. The only reason to open a business is to *make money*. If you don't make a profit, you aren't making money.

Now let's say you have found your niche and you have a steady flow of customers. Your customers love you and your widgets. You have a couple of choices now. You can expand your business to a new location and expand your customer base. You could expand your product line. You could raise or lower prices or stay open longer or on weekends. You *could* settle for the steady income you have, or you could work to increase it. Most business owners wish to increase their income.

Whatever you choose you will also likely need to decide if you wish to continue working 8-to-10-hour days 5 or 6 days a week to maintain your income. If you expand you can't be in both stores at once and if you expand your product line you can't double your work hours. You need employees. Essentially an employee is a person who agrees to perform a task for you in exchange for something, primarily money. On a basic level this can be as simple as "Will you mow my lawn for $5.00?" If you agree to this, then you complete the task and you get your $5.00.

A goal of a businessperson is to be successful enough to continue making a nice income while retiring from the work itself. The only way to do this is to have dedicated employees continuing to run your store. But in the meantime, employees can help to either spread out the work requirement or offer new ways to make more money. Just as you can make a deal with an ink supplier that is mutually beneficial, you make a deal with an employee who is basically in business themselves selling a service to you.

"If you hire me, I can sell more products for you." This is a service a person offers. It is reasonable to view the employer/employee relationship as a business-to-business relationship. As long as it is mutually beneficial then its good business. It really shouldn't get any more complicated than this. As the business owner, you make a list of the things you would prefer not to do yourself or a list of things you need help with, decide what percentage of the profit you currently make (because you still have overhead) you are willing to give to someone else to do those tasks and then you seek out individuals you believe will do those tasks well. The job of the potential employee is to sell their time to you and convince you they will perform your task better than the others applying. As long as the potential employee is satisfied with the percentage of money, they will receive in return all is well.

Imagine this in a business-to-business situation. If you make widgets and I make widget screws, alongside three other screw-making companies, I am offering my widget screws at a certain price, and you decide if you want to buy them from me. Applying for a job is the same concept. Now let's say in this scenario, you choose to buy widget screws from me but find that I am routinely late on shipment, give the wrong quantities or the wrong sizes and when you contact me for support, I delay in getting back with you and typically dismiss you. How long do you think you would continue to give me money to buy my widget screws?

The Free Markets provide competition. There are likely many other screw-makers out there that I am competing against. If you don't like my widget-screws, you can always get them someplace else. Likewise, there are always companies and people looking for widget-screws and you won't be my last customer. Without even a single law in place this system works just fine as human nature will balance the flow. If you engage in poor business practices, then less and less people will want to do business with you and visa verse.

This is also true for employer/employee relationships. If you show up to work late every day, are rude to my customers and routinely perform your job poorly, why would

I continue to pay you to do those things? If I make you work 14-hour shifts, pay you bottom-level wages and routinely bark at you to work harder, why would you continue to offer your services to me for that abuse? In a free market system, there are plenty of other options for me to find new employees or you to find a new employer.

Without getting into the issue of discrimination – this applies to that concept as well. Think in business-to-business terms again. If I have three widget-screw makers to choose from and one is owned by a black person and I don't like black people, then a few things happen: 1) I choose another business 2) I limit my own options to choose from and 3) I might miss out on a great business relationship. Those are choices with consequences. But as a business owner those are my consequences. Affirmative Action in this scenario would force me by law to choose the black-owned business regardless of their quality good or bad. It also forces a potentially good employee to work for someone with small and petty limitations on worldview that conflicts with their own.

When it comes to pay, it is even more simple. After looking at your overhead costs you choose the percentage of the remaining profit to devote to paying an employee. You offer this wage to the employee (price) and the employee decides if it is fair or not. Done. If the employee becomes dissatisfied with the wage, he can attempt to negotiate a better deal or seek a better deal from another employer.

It is in the business-owner's best interest to offer an appealing offer in order to attract a skilled person who will improve their business. As a business owner, you want to improve your business, right? So, wouldn't you prefer someone with more experience or a higher education that leads you to believe they will succeed at this task better? If they disappoint you, shouldn't you be able to replace them with someone else who perhaps will do better?

The savvy employee will develop marketable skills that make her unique so that when she approaches a business, she knows she can negotiate. Since she holds something valuable that the business owner needs, the business owner must offer a good enough incentive for her to dedicate her time and skill to them. This is where benefits come in. "If you work for me, I will offer…"

This used to include things like a contract (3 years guaranteed), salary (a yearly pay vs hourly or daily). access to owner-exclusive deals (stock, investments, etc.), social perks (access to higher society or an impressive title) and so on. Later novel things like health insurance, life insurance and pensions came into play as employers realized that long-term devoted employees made their businesses run more smoothly and therefor made them more money. Investing long-term into a person would mutually benefit both.

In business-to-business deals, benefits include such things as discounts, access to other businesses, long-term partnerships etc. It is better to have a long-term supplier you can count on than to continuously search for a new one. As a result, employees become invested in the business's success. The long-term success of the business means the long-term success of their own career. Earning the trust of the business owner, working hard etc. means promotions, access to better benefits and security. This is how employer/employee relationships should work. Without any laws required.

Customers also enter business agreements with business owners as well. When you walk into a store to buy a widget you are choosing this store and this widget. If the widget breaks or is low quality, then you can find another widget store. In this way, some widget stores realized they could save on production costs by offering lower quality widgets that likely need frequent replacing but can be sold at a cheaper price. Others decided to stick to high quality widgets at higher costs but with better customer loyalty and more reliable future sales. This created diverse variety and it is still reflected today in the $1.00 purse vs the high end $1,000.00+ purse.

What is not often accepted or understood is that the customer is equally responsible for their end of the deal as the business owner is. No one requires them to purchase a widget. As a business owner, you are trying to sell your widget. As a customer, you are looking for the best widget at a price you feel is fair. So, if you read a label that says, "My widget can perform 10 times better than my competitors!" and it does not fulfill said promise you, as a customer, will lose trust or respect for this particular business and will go to another. You might tell your friends too and soon the business owner will lose sales. It is in the business owner's best interest to be transparent, offer a decent product and respect the fair-standards for pricing of his core customer base otherwise he will lose them.

This finely working machine is significantly damaged when regulation and laws come into play that interfere with the businesses and how they function. We think of regulation and laws as ways to keep us safe from unscrupulous business owners. The problem is, we really don't need them to. Looking at some basics we take for granted such as worker protection laws and the minimum wage and you can see how this breakdown occurs.

Wages in particular, stand out the most. Remember how we talked about the employer/employee relationship and how each offer something in return for the other? Well, the minimum wage destroys that. Liberals will demand: "Is it OK to pay $3, $4, or $5 to employees??" The answer is: Yes. If I offer you $3.00 an hour to clean my house and you accept it, then who is harmed? If $3.00 is too low for you then you won't accept the offer.

If I want my house cleaned then I will either raise the rate, continue looking or clean it myself.

The employer must determine his overhead first and then his profit. He has to sell a certain quota of widgets to meet this balance. When he takes on an employee, he is taking on a risk because his business is supported by the work of the employee. If he relies on the employee to close the store every night, count down the cash register, be honest, not steal and reliably do so then he has to keep that employee loyal. This means paying him on time and the agreed upon amount. If the employer finds he isn't able to keep this up, then he lets the employee go. This isn't cold-hearted; It is logical. If you cannot pay your employee because you aren't selling enough to do so, then you terminate the agreement. The employee agreed to perform a service for you for a set price. If you cannot meet that price, then the agreement is off.

A minimum wage takes away the business-owner's ability to balance his own business. If he must pay his employee $9.00 an hour (or probably soon $11.00) then that means he must be able to sell enough to cover his overhead, this wage and still make a profit that makes all of that worth it.

If he is required to offer this wage, just like everyone else, then he loses his competitive edge as well. Let's say your business strategy is to offer a few dollars extra over what your competitors pay their employees. This brings you more employee options to choose from and allows you to be more selective and hopefully get a higher quality employee which will help you increase your sales. If everyone pays $11.00 then you either have to make enough to pay more or you cannot compete, and you will get whoever happens to not be employed elsewhere.

If you cannot meet the $11.00 wage due to your sales, then you cannot have employees and you either work yourself to death to meet that goal and possibly never make anything of your business or you go under. Now zoom out a bit and realize that if $11.00 is the *minimum* wage then that means your suppliers also have to figure out how to meet this number. Usually this means raising the price of goods or services. Now your overhead has also increased. You have a smaller and smaller profit margin and soon being in business at all is pointless.

A minimum wage means employees no longer have to be all that good to get higher pay. Your pool of potential employees that will be motivated to make you more money will weaken. If they all get paid $11.00 no matter what then why should they care to sell more? In the previous system if you sold more, you could get incentives like commissions or raises. Now it doesn't matter how well the business performs as you will get paid either way. Skills themselves become less valuable. There is no benefit to hiring you for your skills if I have to pay everyone the same wage.

Minimums are not supposed to be what is paid forever, but since it makes it more difficult to better the business there is no incentive for the employer to pay higher. If you do sell enough to meet the $11.00 then you don't have to pay any higher. You can take home more profit and keep the same level of employees. Now add to these required benefits such as health insurance. Anyone who walks in the door gets the same benefits as the employee you've had for 10 years.

Soon the purpose of employing someone to improve your business becomes moot. This is where the concept of a "livable wage" causes the most problems. At no point in any of this did the employee's personal choices of how they use their money come into play. Liberals cry about a livable wage and demand that employees who cannot afford rent, food or clothes won't make good employees. Somehow it is the default responsibility of the business owner to provide this for their employees via higher wages. But how would it possibly be the concern or responsibility of the business owner to do this?

Is it a reasonable expectation that, as the business owner, you must pay enough to the widget-screw making business to keep them from going under? If the widget-screw business sells widget-screws for $1.00 a piece but you are on the edge of bankruptcy, should the widget-screw business be required to offer screws to you for $0.10 to keep you afloat? It's absolutely ridiculous.

The assumption is that the business owner has something the employee needs and therefore is morally responsible for providing it. But this isn't true. The business owner is in a mutually beneficial relationship. The employee is not being forced to work there and there is no expectation that this be his only source of income. The employee is, again, offering a business service to the employer. If the terms are not beneficial then he is wasting his time.

A liberal friend of mine once argued: *'You think employers should have run of the economy, that government should be for the corporation and leave people at their tender mercies. The gilded age of the 1800s and early 1900s, and this current gilded age has been some of the worst and most horrible periods of economic injustice in our nation's history. I will not concede to any of your points.*

I fine them offensive, and without any ounce of scholarship. Yes, we're dependent on employment. Such activities pay bills and enable us to live, and as members of society, every person has a duty to contribute to the overall society.'

This is the basic understanding of liberalism towards business. They assume people are entirely helpless and depend on the mercies of others to survive. The very concept that an employee is offering a business service is beyond them. They *believe* that people are subject to government entirely.

This is the most frustrating part of this entire conversation. The assumption that people are dependent on employment is itself offensive. They behave as though businesses, utilities and government exist outside of society and the rest of us are trapped in a bubble between them. Did it occur to them at all that the utility company (water, sewer, electric) were businesses started by people wishing to make a profit on the convenience these services provide? Every business that exists is optional. Every one of them. We do not need any of them.

The problem is that we have become so dependent on convenience we cannot imagine taking care of ourselves. People will stand naked, freezing and starving in the streets complaining about how late the government assistance truck is before they would think to find something to cover up with and hunt for food. There is not a single product or service any of us need to survive. Think about it. Everything is optional. Everything. The only purpose of a business to the customer is to provide an easier and faster way to obtain those optional things. Same friend: *'And my point is that's not what it should be about more than to produce and sell. There are more roles for business to play in society than to offer a product, pay as little as possible to make it, and sell it.'*

This is why we find ourselves a country with half of our population dependent upon the government for survival and the other half paying for their needs via taxes. This is why we have college educated welfare recipients and people satisfied to live on the "minimum" wage for the rest of their lives. By demanding a "livable" wage you take the entire point out of education, skill developing, innovation, personal development and success. But what they do not grasp is that a "livable" wage is impossible.

The moment you determine that a person needs X number of dollars to live comfortably and force that amount onto businesses, prices on everything moves up to compensate and those higher paid minimum wage earners are once again unable to "live" off of their wages. This is why a single paycheck of mine is 3 times more than my grandmother's first annual salary and I cannot afford the lifestyle she had while making less.

I Take Thee to Be My Lawfully Wedded Argument

November 20th, 2013

THIS TOPIC I AM asked about more often than anything else and my answer often holds the entire fate of whatever current or potential relationship I have with the person asking me. I find that absurd. But sadly, we live in a world of extremes right now and it is simply impossible to have a reasonable view on anything. I'm not bitter. Gay marriage or Same Sex Marriage is obviously a very hot topic and it's something that not only provides a clear divide between liberals and conservatives but also gay conservatives and social conservatives. Your position on this topic is a defining position on how you view rights, equality and the future of humanity.

I am fairly neutral on the subject. But I have opinions on both sides. So, this post is not in favor of or in opposition towards same sex marriage. It is just a discussion of some perspectives I have on the issue. I will also provide what I consider to be an alternative solution for my socially conservative friends. First let's talk about what I do not like about the argument.

"Marriage Equality" is a ridiculous term. This is not an issue of "equality" at all. The often mis-used argument for same-sex marriage is that in the past inter-racial marriage was also illegal. If a term like "Marriage Inequality" could be used, inter-racial marriage would be the closest fit to it. We have to understand what equality means. Conservatives and libertarians view equality to mean a level playing field. The individuals may or may not begin at identical positions on the field, but everyone can choose their own distance, direction and new position without unreasonable opposition.

Liberals typically view equality as identical outcome and measure success or failure with how many fail or succeed in an arbitrary outcome. Marriage equality would be best understood as the ability for all qualified individuals to legally become married without unreasonable opposition. Each state establishes its own standards for how it recognizes marriage. This includes age limitations, relation limitations and current marital status. Black and white men and women were already eligible when a law was created to prevent inter-racial marriages. It is also important to note that it was not an issue of recognition but an issue of legality. If an inter-racial couple were to get married the act itself was illegal.

This has no comparison to same sex marriage. Same sex marriage is something *new*. A fair comparison would be legally changing the age limitation. If a state decides to make the age limitation go from 16 to 18, for example, they are adjusting the eligibility standards. Same sex marriage is adding a new standard to the eligibility list by requesting for male/male and female/female be included. It is relevant to understand that the male/male still must be 18, not be blood relations and not currently legally married.

Stating that gay marriage is about equality is not accurate. A gay couple could be married without any legal consequences and certainly without police involvement. There are no arrests made for gay couples attempting to get married. A homosexual person can freely marry someone of the opposite sex. Most gay marriage battles typically begin by a gay couple attempting to obtain a marriage license and being denied. The phrase "making gay marriage legal" is also inaccurate as it is not currently *illegal*. The only difference between two men getting married and a man and a woman getting married is state and federal recognition. This recognition provides certain benefits and legally binds two separate lives together.

Phrases like "Legalize Love" and "Gays should be allowed to marry the person they love" are meaningless since we can already engage in open relationships, and we can already marry the person we love. The only issue is state and federal recognition in legal terms. What I dislike about the pro-gay marriage series of arguments is that they are propaganda rather than arguments. It is intellectually dishonest to shout in outrage that people should "be allowed to love each other." No one is stopping them from loving each other right now. Homosexuality is not illegal. The issue is about changing a cultural appreciation, it's not about equality. There is nothing involved that is equal or unequal in nature. Liberalism tends to fall into mob mentality very quickly and soon you have people sobbing about their "right" to love their partner and screaming in outrage about being second class citizens.

This issue has nothing to do with rights either. There are no "rights" gay people are denied in our society. Gays can vote, we can own guns, we can own property. We are eligible to be elected to political office, we can start our own businesses, we can freely move from state to state unmolested. We have access to the same legal system with the same legal standards. Read the Bill of Rights and pick one that gays are denied. We already have equal rights. What we do not have is equal recognition to the same standards straight people have in all areas.

Hospital visitations, insurance, inheritance, adoption and taxes are not rights. Each issue revolves around either state legal standards or individual company policies. Each can be handled through already-existing processes and do not require federal laws to enforce. Since no gay citizen is denied access to any of those processes then we already have the ability to influence all areas of our society. Liberals like to force their views onto the rest of us so they sue to get their way.

Marriage is not a "human right" either. Marriage is first a religious concept (despite the never-ending arguments about cavemen getting married) that is meant to bind two people together in a specifically religious experience for a specifically religious purpose. Marriage is second a legal matter as described above. A person can freely live happily without being married (Isn't that what feminists have be harping about for the last half century?). Marriage is no more a human right than a driver's license is a human right.

Let's look at it from a different angle.

If you choose to convert to Judaism, you must follow some specific training and rules to do so. You can declare yourself Jewish and practice every Jewish commandment possible – but you will not be recognized as a Jew and will be denied the benefits within the Jewish faith which are only afforded to Jews. Becoming Jewish requires a rabbi to accept you, train you and then perform a ritual. If you complete these tasks, you are Jewish. Different levels of Judaism require different levels of work to be recognized. If you are converted by a Reform rabbi, then an Orthodox rabbi will not consider you to be Jewish.

Now, let's say you decide you want to convert to Judaism, but you want to believe in Jesus too. You approach a rabbi and declare your intentions and the rabbi denies you. Is this an issue of inequality? No. To modify what becoming Jewish is on a fundamental level is something that is understandably undesirable. It honestly doesn't matter how much you feel about the issue or how many arguments you can make that your Judaism is equal in value and practice to their Judaism.

Same sex marriage fundamentally changes the nature of marriage. One man and one woman binding their lives together to be monogamous and commit to a religious lifestyle cannot easily accommodate adding new gender mixes in without significantly changing. Even the concept of a "husband" and a "wife" fundamentally change when you attempt to have two husbands and two wives.

The purpose of traditional modern marriage has significant social implications as well. The intention is for a man and a woman to not only bind themselves to each other for life but do so in a specifically religious way. Our culture requires sex be something only between a married man and a woman and one of the benefits of marriage is having sex on your wedding night. You are expected to only have sex with this one person for the rest of your life and it is intended to be a holy thing. None of this is expected for a same sex couple.

Taking two men and marrying them together is really absurd if you think about it objectively. Nothing about this relationship conforms to any concept of marriage in a religious sense. It is openly defiant of Christianity and Judaism to do so. As someone who is religious (Jewish) and takes my religion seriously, I would be very opposed to changing conversion to include Christian beliefs even if the person or persons wishing to do so were wonderful genuine people.

Christian opposition to changing the very nature of marriage is perfectly reasonable and has nothing to do with hatred of gay people. It is not necessary to argue that many Christians find homosexuality sinful, but that isn't the point. The point is taking something inherently sacred and imposing change onto it in spite of the opposition of those who hold it most sacred is wrong.

My second objection towards the same-sex marriage movement is motivation. In the 80's and 90's liberals, Feminists and gays were loudly decrying marriage as an archaic, patriarchal oppression system. They argued that it dehumanized women, trapped people in limited and dead sexuality and caused most of the social problems we have due to all of this repression. We were trying to remove ourselves from the oppressive stranglehold of Christian tyranny over our culture.

Now all of a sudden, every gay person in America is desperately pleading at the steps of courthouses for the right to engage in said oppressive, archaic, patriarchal, repressive and Christian practice as a way to fulfill their very being. Certainly, gays have matured from our sexual revolution-style attempts at shocking the establishment and many thousands have settled into long-term relationships with children etc. But, as I will discuss, the things those families need are reasonable and often already-in-place legal issues. The ones protesting in the streets seem to just want it because someone told them they can't have it.

There is a mentality that if you have 10 clubs and 9 of them offer a variety of environments and experiences but 1 is exclusive in some way – everyone will desperately want in that 1 club. So much of the same sex argument is defiance and aggressive forcing of those who do not agree with you to submit. There is, for example, absolutely no reason for gay couples to legally force Christian bakeries to cater their weddings outside of a Liberal religious obsession with forcing their will at sword point.

What I support about same sex marriage is common sense legal accessibility. I know a Lesbian couple where one gave birth to their children while the other worked to support the family. In my state their relationship had no legal status and so the non-birth mother has no legal rights to her children. That is just silly to me. They also could not get "family" discounts at the local gym either which was just an idiot business move since they were both wealthy.

Most limitations are just legal hurdles, and most can be worked around. Some things like taxes or legal relationship status (guardian) are not as easy to work around. We have tools to deal with businesses who don't recognize same sex partners if we choose, and legal issues are just legislation. Nearly everything else can be formed into place – it just isn't automatic like it is for married couples.

Devil's advocate argument:

I have a strong relationship with two older people with children around my age. They are like my family. I often find myself in the place of a son and they often fill the roles of my parents. We have a very strong emotional bond. Legally we are strangers. If they died and did not write me into the will, I have no legal claim to their estate. If I die, they have no influence over my burial or my estate either. Like "husband" and "wife" they can never be my "mother" or "father." Our emotional relationship may be identical – but it is simply not legally. It is not an issue of equality that their children do have those automatic privileges and I do not. If my bond was much closer than their children's, it is irrelevant to the legal situation.

Now they could write me into their will with an equal standing to their children just as I could make them my legal representatives for death decisions etc. Just because the non-birth mother in my beginning statement raised and loved the children does not influence, at all, their legal relationship to her. This is why purely emotional arguments are pointless. It does not matter how much two men love each other. We need a legal status in order to obtain legal benefits. Fortunately, we live in a country which allow the citizens to influence their laws.

The other downside to the emotion argument is that it redefines marriage in a significant way. Just like my parent/child scenario, if love is all the defines a right to marriage, then there are some serious questions we need to address. If the standard is "love" then any denial of social and legal status based on love would be discrimination no matter how absurd it might be. While gay advocates dismiss the slippery-slope argument – it is valid. People have the capability to love with equal passion and validity: multiple partners, wide age ranges, inanimate objects, animals and fictional characters. While there is always a fallback argument of "consent" being involved – this is just another form of discrimination. "Two consenting adults" is arbitrary at best and is temporary as psychology evolves and changes the significance of romantic relationships across the board.

Limiting the number of partners is discriminatory. Limiting the age of partners is discriminatory. The list can continue on and if you have ever hear of you know that people are capable of strongly defending their right to love balloons with the same defiance as men defending their right to love other men.

In a free society, this is perfectly fine for the most part – but legally recognizing these statuses becomes tricky. How exactly would we navigate 5 partners with 5 sets of children from 5 other partners all married together when one wishes to divorce?

Here is my perspective and my proposed solution:

From a traditional Jewish perspective marriage serves two purposes: to benefit society and to build a religious significant family with easy to track heritage and a moral and sexually restrained relationship. Jews marry other Jews in a Jewish wedding and promise to build a Jewish life together according to Torah. But non-Jews? They can pretty much do what they want.

Just like non-Jews can eat ham and we don't care, non-Jews can get married any way they choose. All we care about is a peaceful society. If same sex marriage benefits outside society – so be it. Just leave us alone about it. Gay people getting married isn't harming society. Marriage is generally positive on social structures and there is no socially negative impact.

Most of the opposition comes from religious Christians who feel marriage is a unique and very significant contract between man and G-d and must be sacred. They view the radical changes as a direct attack on their religious experience and the experience they hope for all people. They feel that if marriage is watered down to a mere legal ceremony, then it will lose all significance for everyone.

What I argue is that marriage was watered down when it became secular. People can already get married without any religious significance even though they still hold onto the social constraints that are only relevant under religious circumstances such as monogamy. Marriage and divorce already dominate most of our society and people seem to view marriage more like a prom than a significant experience. People live together for years anyways, and sex is a part of everyday life without the same "wait until marriage" significance. We socially mock people who stay virgins for marriage now.

A still-held argument is the idea that accepting gay marriage will bring a social acceptance of homosexuality which many forms of Christianity oppose. Gays are already socially accepted as is a general feeling of sexuality existing outside of marriage. Most people know gay people and the idea that gays are harmful to society is opposed on a large scale. Most realize it is a pretty silly argument and we have better information now. Certainly, when gay men were only understood to be pedophiles or seedy characters hiding in alleys and the development of HIV/AIDS was new it made sense to worry about the social consequences of children being exposed to that. But obviously now we understand homosexuality differently and see the wide variety of ways it is expressed in human interactions.

Our society already associates marriage with love and therefore is sympathetic to the idea of same sex partners loving each other. This isn't something worth fighting against. It is one thing to attempt to influence society and prevent unwanted changes but it's another to have the perception that you are "taking away" something people find fair and just. Even though gay advocates are arguing the wrong things and, in my opinion, taking the wrong approaches to influence society to their views – average people view same sex marriage as a natural evolution of human acceptance.

The solution, in my opinion, is not the continual duality of opposition and support. Like Jews, Christians should consider religious marriage to be something sacred and unique for them as it is currently only truly appreciated by them. Secular marriage is like secular Christmas or secular education. If a person wishes to take part in the legal benefits of marriage, then they can get a marriage license from the state and hold a religious wedding. It is completely ok to have a purely religious wedding without any legal recognition as well.

I don't think this is giving up as I feel traditional marriage proponents are pushing a rock up a hill. Even if you had a 90% public vote in favor of banning same sex marriage, proponents would just file lawsuit after lawsuit until they found a judge to overturn it. They are pushing the rock down the hill at the same time you are pushing it up the hill. The sometimes-knee-jerk reaction to liberal aggression can be an equal force of opposition.

Conservatives as a whole are gay-friendly. I rarely even encounter negative views about homosexuality as a concept. There is, however, a strong reaction to the way gay advocates push their views. Sometimes we get caught up in the need to oppose the argument rather than actually opposing the argument. Sometimes retreat is the best strategy. Let the rock roll down the hill and them with it. Meanwhile build your own schools, your own communities and focus on building a beautiful and uniquely holy religious marriage concept in those communities.

You can be legally ordained as multiple forms of a "minister." This does not change the significance of your minister or priest or pastor or their authority and influence. I feel the same thing just needs to happen within Christianity and marriage. The benefits of this will be a true form of religious-based marriage that religious people can find authentic which will widen the gap between secular legal marriage and religious marriage. Christians can feel confident in their experience in holding to tradition and it will be more significant and meaningful to them just like Jewish traditions are to us.

Conclusion

I support making legal avenues for different types of relationships more accessible since many of the restrictions now are based on the assumption of a religious standard. I accept that this will be complicated as relationship styles evolve but I feel there is always room for the voters to voice their needs to improve their own society.

I do not support the aggressive bully tactics gay advocates often use to force their way. Christian cake makers should not be legally forced to participate in gay weddings.

Churches, religious-owned parks and event places should not be legally forced to participate in gay weddings. I don't like government interference in how people feel, think or what they believe, and I really dislike the use of our court system to overturn votes when a minority is displeased with the results.

I absolutely hate the nonsense propaganda about "Marriage Equality" and I wish people could argue the issue honestly rather than infuse the situation with so much emotion no one can think clearly. These are solvable problems with absolutely no need draw a line and play enemies. I respect marriage as a religious tradition with sacred meaning and a serious commitment to a religious lifestyle. I do not like it when people hijack religion to force their own point of view or to prove a point. Gay marriage is a significant step in our society, and I cannot say whether it is good or bad. I feel that we must, however, find a way to be reasonable about the situation rather than playing capture the flag with lawsuits and court decision.

What Do You Call a Gay Conservative?

November 30th, 2013

"Gay Conservative" is kind of like "Black Conservative", it serves a point but not a very good one. To be clear, Conservatives in general do not require subgroup identification. As far as any Conservatarian (Conservative + Libertarian) is concerned, I share views with them, and we stand together one some fundamental issues. None of them care that I am gay. This shocks and disorients liberals. Liberalism has convinced all of us that the only way to prove diversity works is to require every citizen to carefully write out a nametag with their appropriate subgroup in society and where it for everyone to see. I need a bigger name badge.

I am Jewish. I am gay. Neither of those things directly intersect with my views on taxes or national security. But in order to provide some frame of reference when discussing anything with a liberal I must explain myself very clearly. Typically, any person who fits into a checkbox on a diversity sheet is a wild, rebel radical if they choose to identify with Conservatives. We find ourselves defending our motivations, defending our integrity and most commonly, responding to accusations that we are crazy.

A *Huffington Post* article titled *Dan Savage Reacts To Gay Conservative Group Endorsing Romney With Explicit Tweet,* by quoting Savage's tweet: *"The GOP's house faggots grab their ankles, right on cue: .... Pathetic"*[1]

I routinely fend off the *"OMG you're a GAY Republican??"* reaction enough to deeply sigh and respond with a clearly annoyed..." *yeeess*" at this point. It's so boring and predictable. It is also a strong indicator of just how bigoted liberals truly are. Black people, women, Latinos, Gays, Jews – all of us are clearly too stupid to think for ourselves. As a gay person, my personality, viewpoints and values are already predetermined by liberal standards. If I step outside of that box there must be something terribly wrong!

My favorite is the idea that I am somehow just not educated enough to know better. You know, if I just stopped watching *Faux* News long enough, I might see different perspectives of the world. The nicer ones try to reach out and hold my hand telling me of the wonderful world outside of my tiny little cage where the mean Christians put me. I am just a sad example of Stockholm Syndrome and I desperately want my oppressors to love me so I will do anything for even a weak nod in my direction! Don't I know that they will turn and toss me out of the boat as soon as I'm not needed any longer?

Somehow, I am supposed to believe that the people who openly listen to my point of view, share their experiences and opinions with me, respect my agreement and disagreement with them and others, retweet and like my comments and generally never fail to be pleasant to me are the hidden enemy and the people who routinely mock me, dismiss me and claim I am dangerous for thinking differently are my true friends.

Again, the assumption is that my sexuality overrides everything else. For many gay people this is absolutely true. I can remember having arguments with gay friends over Obama and Romney where after agreeing that Obama's policies would destroy the economy, limit personal freedoms and send us into a nose-dive as a society they still insisted they would support him anyways because he got rid of DADT and supported Gay Marriage.

If you ask me its Gay Democrats who are the truly brainwashed here. They routinely ignore gay-issue flip-flopping from Democrats and are so comfortable in their biased view of Republicans as the evil plotting Christian oppressors they simply don't care enough to think outside of that box. While I am assumed to be uneducated, lost in my desperate need for approval and trapped by my own self-hatred – it's really the liberal gays who are trapped. They all say the same things, have the same argument points and are always willing to personally attack you when losing said argument. They are the ones who will wish you a painful death of AIDS. They are the ones who determine your entire worth as a human based on what they perceive to be your political point of view. They are the ones who will terminate friendships, mock you openly and try to destroy your image and name as revenge for your heresy.

Even social conservatives who are not shy about expressing negative views on homosexuality in general are kind and respectful of me. They do not hold up their hand and dismiss my entire argument or point of view because I am gay. I lose gay friends when I "come out" as a Conservative and libertarian. My conservatarian friends couldn't care less about my sexuality.

Identity politics place people into tightly defined niches and force us to defend or oppose parties, people, laws etc. based on how they interact with our niche. If a candidate is 90% better for us as a whole but doesn't support that 10% based around our niche, we are willing to support the 10% good candidate who does. People voted for Obama because of what he represented as a concept. Being the "First Black President" in capital letters was more important than who he was as a leader or a person. Gays love him because he pretends to love them back. Conservatives are just honest with us. I am open about my support for same-sex marriage, but I would never consider a candidate as positive *just because* he or she supported legal accommodation for same sex couples.

I tend to keep up the "Gay Conservative. Republican, Libertarian, Tea Party" title because it is a necessary reminder to *other* people that liberals do not control the message. There are many perspectives out there and the most valuable part of a person is their ability to think for themselves. I am not some kid who never had exposure to different points of views and now only tightly cling to my conservative views because I am too afraid to step outside of my dark cave.

In fact, it's the other way around. I was a kid never exposed to anything, but liberal views and I held onto them until logic, reason and overwhelming evidence forced me to let go. Conservative and libertarian views make more sense to me. They are what is left over when you remove all the nonsense. I am a conservatarian *because* I forced myself to understand *why* I believed what I did, not in spite of it.

The Wrong Direction

December 30th, 2013

I AM FINANCIALLY UNSTABLE because of my choices, period. This is the most difficult statement to make in our society, I think. We have spent so long blaming the wealthy for the condition of the poor that we have never truly evaluated what poverty means. Since I was a kid, I have heard nothing but emotional efforts to help the poor and ever-growing anger towards the rich as a result of the continued needs of the poor. Buying chicken hotdogs at a dollar store and adding a little more cash advance to my account to make sure I don't go overdrawn it would be assumed I would agree with this perspective. But I know better.

I am probably classified as upper-lower class. I am not middle class, and I am not in poverty because I make a few thousand more a year than the minimum, but I certainly have been in the category of "the poor" for my entire life. I qualify for several government programs. I grew up in a trailer with my single father who never made more than $25,000 a year after 25 years of service. I make a little more than that now. I struggle to balance the money I have with what has to be spent and I am in fairly hopeless debt due to my student loans.

Am I victim of a cruel society dominated by the greedy rich? No. I am the product of my own choices with finances, education and career choices.

Here is what I think the core of poverty in our country is based on:

- Dependence on debt

- Misunderstanding of what money is

- Absurd work/value expectations

- Poor priority planning

- Poor future planning

- An obsessive need to satisfy immediate needs

If you make $1000 a month and your expenses are $500 a month you have enough to live on. People will argue against this, but it's true. The reason it doesn't work is because of everything I listed above. People have debt, late bills and spend money without priority planning at all. We have the expectation of equal lifestyle across the board with no concept of the value or expectations of said lifestyle. This is why a person's $120 phone bill will get paid but their electric gets turned off.

The standard argument is that poor people are paid too little and because they do not receive a "livable wage" they are unable to survive. I argue that any wage is "livable" as long as your priorities and expectations are accurate. Just like you cannot walk out in a speedo when you are overweight and expect the same kind of positive attention a bodybuilder receives, you cannot expect to have a lifestyle above what you can afford. We find this concept both cruel and preposterous.

We are looking in the wrong direction to find a solution and we are certainly targeting our anger at the wrong group of people. Instead of disapprovingly shaking our heads at how a person could spend $5,000 on a purse or $500 on a meal, we should be appalled at the reality of people on welfare spending $500 on Christmas presents. The waste and mismanagement is what is truly disgraceful and what our society should be attempting to correct with public pressure. The rich should be our role models, not the villain in the story. Making money and maintaining an expensive lifestyle one can afford should be viewed as brilliance rather than wasteful arrogant evil.

This is one of the issues where I can draw a clean line between Liberalism and Conservative/Libertarianism. Liberals look at a poor person working 60 hours a week in a low paying job as the height of nobility and the rest of us wonder why that person isn't striving for bigger and better things. Liberalism would gasp in horror that children wouldn't receive gifts on Christmas or that their parents wouldn't have TV. The idea that a luxury exists does not mean everyone has a moral right to access it equally. The absurdity of how we view the usage of money demonstrates why we live in such a strange world where people make tons of money but are desperately poor.

Take for instance credit. Credit should only be available to those who have demonstrated financial responsibility over time with a specific institution, say a bank. A bank is willing to lend you money and you promise to pay it back within a certain amount of time.

What logic would suggest that a person who cannot afford to pay the loan back should be given the loan? This is not a moral argument; it is a logical one. How is it morally just to give money to a person who cannot afford to pay it back and then spend the rest of that person's life chasing them down for it? "People deserve houses." But if they cannot afford the house, how is it fair or righteous to put them in a financial situation which will ultimately result in them losing said house?

Liberalism focuses on the emotional impact of the immediate situation. It is unfair that a person and their family do not own a house; they cannot get credit. Now the children are crying. This is an outrage! We must pursue Justice! Force the banks to give them credit to buy a house they cannot afford! Our work is done. Conservatism places the responsibility on the individual with the understanding that they have unlimited potential depending on how they use the resources they have available.

Our current plan, thanks to endless liberal wailing about "fairness," allows a person to accumulate obscene amounts of debt before they have any ability to set up a financial plan to pay for it. People are given credit with absolutely no logical reason to believe they can handle it. People are also constantly being told they deserve things and therefore use the credit, or "free money," and spend the rest of their lives paying it off. I would bet that the majority of people who fall into the category of "poverty" have a great deal of debt in the form of credit cards and loans.

Liberals want us to believe there is a huge swath of people born into abject poverty and due to the influences of greedy rich people they never have any opportunity to escape it. The only options they have are government programs designed to support them. They completely ignore the reality that every single person has the same ability to achieve the lifestyle they want – if they make the right choices. Education, opportunity, and other "income inequality" arguments always take the responsibility and the freedom away from the individual.

I remember being in a college class with my professor talking about how he walked past drug dealers and homeless people every day from school. He lamented: "How can we expect any child to escape this when it's all they see?" When I asked him how he managed to do it he dismissed it as a "white privilege" point of view. Apparently, I was viewing the experience through distorted "white privilege" eyes that deceptively assume people can make choices to better their situations.

In any discussion on poverty, you will hear about all of the negative environmental and sociological influences that prevent people from achieving. This ranges from young pregnancy to drug use to poorly funded education systems. The solution is always more school funding, more social programs and higher taxes on the rich.

I like to point out that we spend a great deal of tax money on food programs already and yet we have a never-ending hunger problem. This, to me, is demonstrated by two things:

- Even with access to food cards we still have a large hungry population

- People with food cards do not improve their food situations

Somehow, we still have hunger. The question is why? Why would we have people who need food when we have a taxpayer funded government food program? The other question is why do we have unhealthy, obese welfare recipients who still need a monthly food card income? The assumption is that if people just need food and we have food programs then every person should be able to access food and as a result be healthier and require less and less need for the program over time. But the reality is that those who use the program do not make better food choices, acquire food stores or balance their financial lives to no longer need the food program.

If you tell me that you don't make enough money to buy food and pay for your essential bills and I give you money to cover all food costs – shouldn't you now have extra money to cover essential bills? Over time you should accumulate the money you were spending on food until you can both pay for your bills and buy food as you no longer need the card to fill the gap. Unfortunately, people see it as "free money" and use it to buy whatever they immediately need in food and never think farther than the next month when it refills.

This is the same with debt. Debt should be to either assist in a very large purchase or as an emergency fund available if needed. People see debt as another form of money.

Money that does come in is not considered any farther than its immediate use. Ideally a person should look at the money they earn and then decide what bills they can take on and still have money left over which should continue to accumulate over time. This way if they never earn more money, they will always have a growing amount available in case of an emergency or to upgrade their lifestyle once it is sufficient. What we do is spend every cent we have and spend money we do not have in the form of debt. Our income does not change but our bill requirement continues to rise. The higher it goes the more debt we need to fill in the gaps and so on. We assume there will always be income and eventually – somehow – the debt will disappear.

Instead of prioritizing our monthly needs in a way that secures us against disaster and then keeping the rest in savings, we buy what we want at the moment until we run out. This is a mindset and is now a culture we have created. We have faith in future money without any plan to acquire it and as long as politicians demand more and more money be taken from the rich to give to us in the form of government programs, bailouts and banks are forced to give us credit we have no incentive to think otherwise.

People who are very wealthy plan their money alongside their income potential and strive to continue improving.

What about education, opportunity and "white privilege"?

We assume that rich people had advantages that allowed them to be successful while poor people are trapped and unable to succeed. But our history proves this wrong. Look at our grandparent's generation and look at their education and opportunities. Look at black people pre-1960's and see how even under intense racial discrimination individuals succeeded under impossible situations. People went to school with dirt floors and no running water and the reason they succeeded was because they understood that the purpose of education is to give you tools to go out into the world and have an advantage.

My grandmother believed education was her key to success, so she went after it with force. Being a poor girl in a large family living on a dirt road in the mountains of West Virginia in the 1930's and 40's did not stop her from building a life where she secured her own future through her own choices. Children today in the poorest of schools have more access to education than any children in the history of the world. The lack is not funding, creative teaching or diversity. The lack is student appreciation of education.

This is why it doesn't matter how many kids are pushed through graduation without the ability to read beyond the 5th grade level or how many are pushed into college degrees – the success rate doesn't improve.

What about environmental situations like abuse, single motherhood, inner city life etc?

This is going to piss people off, but when did getting pregnant become the same thing as getting the flu? Again, teenage pregnancy has nothing to do with education, awareness or available contraception in classrooms. It has to do with future planning and the appreciation of individual responsibility. A boy and girl who believe they must equip themselves with the tools to stand out and get good jobs so they can build a secure life that allows them to pursue happiness through financial freedom are not going to "accidentally" get pregnant.

Kids do stupid things. But that's because kids have no concept of cause and effect with their lives. No one tells them about how they can control anything. This is true for drug use, crime or any other activity that can harm their futures. The reason kids engage in these behaviors is because they do not value their own lives or their own futures.

People believe getting wealthy comes through luck or through cheating. Poor people believe that "one day" they will have "enough" money. Kids assume getting money will just happen. We all are still waiting for Oprah to show up, point to us and shout "YOU GET A CAR!!"

Wealthy people seem to understand that they must act every day to secure their lifestyles. At a certain point, of course, things like water bills and electricity become less important worries, but they are more responsible for their money than anyone else. They also have a huge tax burden as well.

Instead of demonizing their success and bitterly complaining about how they use their money, we should be admiring their ability to control their lives and build wealth. Instead of expecting them to give us what we want or need because they have more than they need, we should be studying them and copying what they do. People who are wealthy are people who broke the mold. They are the 45-year-old muscular guys with abs. They are unusual and they have gotten where they are due to hard work and smart thinking. We need to admire them and strive to be like them.

More importantly we need to recognize that we don't need to be them. There is a place where you can only pay rent so low and manage debt so much. You can improve yourself to get a better job but unless you made good decisions early on it becomes tougher to stand out. You have to be willing to take risks too. There is a point where you may barely make enough to cover what you absolutely need. Ideally this is the argument for government programs – to help you fill in gaps until you can get past it. But if you focus on all aspects from how you spend your money to how you handle debt and so on you can rise above it.

The most impactful thing a rich person could do for a poor person would not be to pay all of their bills or hand them money. The most powerful and empowering thing they could do would be to teach that person how to take control of their own finances. Taking control of your own financial life is far more important than having someone else take on your financial burden. Wealth doesn't mean you have to own 5 houses and your own jet. It means building your life so that your work pays for the lifestyle you love and can afford.

Sadly, we are growing more dependent on others to secure our futures for us. We sit and watch people protest for higher minimum wages. We elect politicians who promise us more entitlements. We believe it is morally righteous to "help the poor" by taking money from the rich. The only people who will ever rise above where they are will be those willing to step outside of the crowd and make it happen with everything they have. It's not luck. It's not greed. It's not fairness. Its personal responsibility. The poor already have all the resources they need to experience financially secure and fulfilled lives. It's something I am learning more about every day. I will get there eventually.

Infinite Gender

February 23rd, 2014

FACEBOOK HAS MADE AN interesting decision to expand its gender selection options. If you raised an eyebrow trying to grasp how that could be more than two, you're in for a surprise. The sheer level of absurdity is hilarious: "A trans man is a girl born with girl parts but who identifies as a boy, but who still wants to be with a boy just like she was a girl. Ira [Warren Beatty and Annette Benning's college-age daughter is a trans man.] goes on to say she is a binary trans man. Binary refers to those who can accept living as a man or a woman no matter what they were "assigned" at birth."[2]

On Ira's personal blog, he commented further in an article titled *Why Chaz Bono Is a Misogynist Who Does Not Represent Us:* "Chaz [Bono referenced in the article] is erasing the experience of trans men who don't need top surgery. He's reinforcing this cissexist idea that having breasts that you intend to keep equals being a woman, which we know from experiences of many non-op, non-binary and intersex people is just not true."[3]

According to *Seven Questions About Transgender Issues You Were Afraid to Ask* we, as a society, are currently under siege from rampant cis-sexism. If you have never heard of this condition and may not have realized that you suffer from cis-sexism yourself, allow me to explain. First, what is the "Cis" in this discussion? This refers to a gender-identity known as Cisgender. A Cisgender person identifies with the gender they were born with. So, if you were born male and you identify as male then you are a Cisgender person.

Apparently Transgender people decided it was necessary to create a new category for everyone else and that's what they now call us. Look for this as a new standard liberals will wish to force upon the masses (think "Undocumented American"). Along with "Transwoman" as opposed to "woman" for those who have transitioned, liberals have found yet even more complicated ways to divide people and create even more unnecessary tension amongst us. A quick Google search reveals that "cis-sexism/cissexism" and "cissexist" are being used with common frequency on Left-leaning websites. I guess they assumed you already knew this, otherwise you are just another bigoted ignorant redneck.

Naturally, cis-sexism refers to what I suppose most people (normal people) view as 'abnormal' in terms of gender identity politics. I apologize, the use of 'normal' and 'people' together to describe those who identify with the gender they were born with was very cissexist of me. This is how the 'Seven Questions' article defines cissexism: "Cissexism means assuming that everyone has this same experience, and that anyone who doesn't is inferior or somehow deviates from what's normal."

Incidentally, how exactly would you explain the experience that most people have? How would you describe an experience that *deviates* from said experience? By definition a person born male who believes they are female and radically changes their body to conform to this view is not *normal* and is actively *deviating* from *normal* since the most common experience is to identify and remain in your birth gender. What liberals are telling us is that anyone who is not actively questioning or changing their gender identity is a cissexist and should be shunned.

An example of cis-sexism from the article is described as such: "Where I fear cis-sexism is as a lesbian partner of a trans woman I fear that I won't be seen as a real lesbian, on account of the fact that I'm not with a real woman. It prevents me from going out and getting involved in the scene. I won't go out to a lesbian club unless I am certain that she'll be accepted. I just don't want to be in that situation. This is where I think loads of feminists get it completely wrong. Cis-sexism is just another form of elitism and acts at excluding people by virtue of their past physical history, how is that fair?"[4] Feel free to read that again if it took you a minute to categorize everyone involved properly. If you paused and thought 'what the hell?' while reading and considered for a moment how utterly absurd both the situation and the emotional concern was, you might suffer from cis-sexism. Feel ashamed!

Now, full disclosure: I am technically a transgender person. When I was a child, I strongly identified with being a girl, wanted to be a girl and often behaved, dressed and fantasized as a girl. In my early 20's I even pursued therapy to begin the process of gender reassignment. I was diagnosed as transgendered then. I ended up not going through with it then because I was not 100% committed and felt it was too overwhelming. Over time I realized that I enjoyed my physical gender and my desire to be female was more associated with a strong desire to be accepted and appreciated by men rather than anything else. My spirituality allowed me to understand that I could have a female spirit in a male body or any number of other possibilities.

Interestingly I have a gender title called *Transfeminine* which I discovered on the list of 56 Facebook gender options which summarizes all that nicely. Interestingly there is no firm theory as to why people like me may later reevaluate their gender identity and become, essentially, cisgender. I understand and appreciate the confusion, frustration and desire to be the opposite gender. I have absolutely no negative views of people who take this path and gender transformation is such that a person can fully embrace a new gender as fully as they can a new religion if they chose to do so. I am not interested in the intellectual argument of whether this is a delusional disorder similar to paranoia or delusions of grandeur where a person strongly believes or feels something that only exists in their own mind. I don't eat shrimp because I feel strongly G-d told me not to in a book. I'm not judging.

People manipulate their bodies in many ways and to many extremes and this interferes with how they are treated in public. Extreme body building women, for example, experience different struggles in the workplace, dating and going to the mall than average-shaped women as do very obese women. Changing your body to better suit your personal desires can be fulfilling but it is unreasonable to expect 100% acceptance everywhere you go.

The original concerns around the transitioning period, often several years in the making, focused on violence, workplace discrimination, medical discrimination etc. This demonstrates how important gender is in our society, especially for men who interact with women. Masculinity and sexuality are very complex, but it is well understood that if a man pretends to be a woman to engage sexually with a straight man, he may find out his reaction can be very violent. The reasons are equally as complex, but besides deception, the fear of hidden homosexuality, violation etc. and the intimate experience a man has with a woman to which he does not express to a man can cause a very volatile scenario.

Transgender people have long been associated with this deception. During the 1980's and 90's it was a theme on TV of passable transgender women and the male romantic interests they dealt with. In many ways, it is viewed as one of those most repulsive experiences a man could engage in and is often viewed as a source of humor as well. The idea of a man who is genuinely a woman inside and goes through the transition to become a woman and therefore should be treated as a woman in every way is something alien to us.

This doesn't mean the female to male version has it any easier, but it is generally less of an issue for a woman to have masculine qualities and the physical transition is often so outwardly convincing it's not disruptive in everyday life. While there are many variations of sexual expression, female to male transitions can have a more receptive female dating pool in the spectrum of lesbian and bisexual women who appreciate sexual fluidity. Even if a female to male person engages with a fully heterosexual woman, the idea is much easier to embrace.

Male to female transitions are often homosexual in nature and the target romance pool are straight men which is why the experience is so different. The physical transition can be much less convincing, and the transition time frame can cause a physically female person to still have male genitalia which creates a uniquely difficult experience for all parties involved. Straight men can feel "tricked" into sex and revealing the transition may lead to complete termination of the relationship, so it causes secrets and tension. Transition at work can be complicated if you begin as one gender and show up to work dressed as the other. Not all employers have been comfortable with this.

More recent complaints are now focused on bathroom usage and what pronouns are appropriate to use and when. As usual, liberalism takes something the general public is uncomfortable with, defines themselves by supporting it and then rabidly force laws to require compliance with their views on the issue. They create labels, "isms" and feverishly write articles bemoaning the "intolerance" they encounter while trying to change the entire culture by force. A Huffington Post article titled *Trans 101: A Primer for the Ignorant and the Intolerant* demonstrates this smug attitude perfectly.

Instead of exploring the idea of gender identity being something some struggle deeply with or even a biological malformation that may cause female mental responses in a male body etc. and allowing the public to understand a condition that can be resolved as was attempted in the late 90's with some success, transgender people choose to now be righteously indignant, demanding and as separate as possible as they lecture us all on how they are being victimized by us. Looking at the very title of the above article we can see the seething bigotry spewed at anyone who does not fully embrace the writer's personal view on the subject.

How would anyone possibly know a genetically male person fully dressed as a woman was entering a public restroom for women and then be horribly offended or call the police? They wouldn't. There is no logical reason why this would be a problem unless he lifted up his dress and peed in the sink in front of a grandmother and her granddaughter.

But liberals define themselves by living in an utterly tolerant society and finding ways to push it to the limit just to prove a point and so they announce to a store manager their current condition and demand to use the restroom of their choice causing a ruckus. If they are denied at that point they call the ACLU, the news stations and sob about how oppressed they are.[5]

Soon they file lawsuits and demand all stores be required by federal law to allow gender-non-specific individuals to use whichever restroom they prefer, and conservatives respond with a backlash suddenly imagining men in dresses around young girls in bathrooms and/or to the completely unnecessary further regulation of industry to absurd PC nonsense and file counter lawsuits or proactively ban it altogether. Before you know it, LGBT organizations are sounding the alarms over the evil Right-wing oppressing poor transgendered people and the cycle continues.

Displays like this further embed the idea that transgender people are mentally unstable and merely part of the liberal freak-show concept that anything goes in any way at any time with no limitations and that anyone who gets in their way will be stomped to death. A Huffington Post article by the same author as above titled: *Pardon Andrea Jones* laments: "Andrea Jones, a Tennessean trans woman, was arrested for baring her breasts in protest of the state's decision that she be considered legally male, despite the state's indecent exposure laws not barring exposure of the chests of those considered legally male. It was a brilliant, simple, visceral, logical idea. She proved that while the state may refuse to dignify her identified sex, they cannot bring themselves to ignore it, either."

And this particularly interesting logic: "I wonder what would happen if, in every town and county where there were at least a dozen trans people (so, almost anywhere), groups of trans people got together to ensure their safety as they used public accommodations. I wonder what would happen if the owners of health clubs and dressing rooms and other sex-segregated public accommodations, instead of being able to marginalize one or two very silent and frightened trans people, were faced with two groups of trans people — one group of trans men and one group of trans women — that simply said to whomever had authority over the public accommodation in question, "Where do we go to change?"

I think any rational person would rather have trans women in the women's room and trans men in the men's room. Of course, if they clung to their cissexism, they could enjoy sending to the women's room half a dozen hairy, bearded, gravelly-voiced people who smell like men, call themselves men, are called men by the people they like and respect, and engage in the kind of talk that tends to happen between men in the change room, but who have vaginas. And they could enjoy explaining that to their children, should they bring those children into a clothing-optional change room, since, you know, they really believe that trans men are just women, and vice versa."[6]

While liberals celebrate their brilliance in this, they also manage to prove my point: who would possibly know there was an issue at all unless you made it one? After witnessing Piers Morgan be destroyed by these people over his horrific offense of referring to a transwoman as once being a boy, we see the newest stage of liberal force: aggressive social backlash to any perceived deviation from their singular view of what is "correct."

Transgender people have collectively decided they want to be considered their preferred gender from birth as though it somehow validates their narrative of *being* the preferred gender rather than accepting the common-sense realization that they were, in fact, one gender physically until they chose to change it. This is not in any way offensive.

For some reason, something as innocent as pointing out a before and after in a journey of a person's life has become hate speech. Instead of demonstrating the journey as something they have embraced and celebrated, they choose to force compliance on the false narrative that they never changed their gender at all. The logic is that because people have always viewed gender change as cosmetic and something along the lines of tattooing your entire body to look like a zombie or a lizard, it has been decided that in order to give "dignity" to people who change their gender it must be something never again mentioned, even though all they do is point it out.

In a *Think Progress* article titled: *Janet Mock Schools Piers Morgan On How To Tell Transgender Stories, Mock*, a transgender activist scolds Morgan: *"MOCK: Before commercial break, we had a lovely conversation, and then all of a sudden you said, "...who was formerly a man." I was a baby. I was assigned male gender because of the appearance of my genitals. As I grew up, I discovered my girlhood, I discovered my womanhood, and I proclaimed and defined myself for myself."*[7]

Take for example "Transwoman" vs "woman." If it offends you that a person would recognize and point out that you were once male and transitioned into a female physically, why would you insist on a separate gender title that tells everyone that you were in fact once male and transitioned into a female? If you define your identity by telling everyone how you were once a boy and became a woman via your never-ending demands for "equality" due to said choice, why would you cry out about "ignorance!" and "intolerance!" when people merely state it as a fact, while never interrupting your equality in the process?

So, you are telling me that you were born male, decided for yourself you were female, chose to transform your body to now appear female and brand your entire identity as a "Transwoman" who transitioned from male to female, but it offends you if a person states you were once male? How do you expect to be treated naturally as a woman if you continue to insist on demanding everyone appreciate your transition from male to female and then call your liberal attack dogs when they describe said transition?

The definers of "cissexism" are wrong. Cissexism is not elitism, liberalism is elitism. Liberals demand that they alone define reality and all who question them must be punished. Only they can declare what is right and what is wrong and all else are merely ignorant bigots who should be scorned. This is all a side effect of the liberal obsession with taking something they believe to be true, foisting it on the public and dealing with independent thinkers protesting the invasion. If you decide to do something that is socially risky or even unacceptable there are consequences. I agree that transitioning is not a "choice" in the same area as full body tattoos, but it is a choice still. Just like bodybuilders choose to build their bodies far beyond normal proportions, there is no reasonable expectation of pure neutrality in the reaction. Fair or not, if you are male and you transition physically to female your experience is not going to be neutral and your personal relationships will rely on building trust and not demanding all people treat you or view you exactly as you choose to be viewed.

As evidenced by the recent Facebook decision to add 56 gender options, there is an absurdity growing between personal expression and definition and the expectation that others will accept you exactly as you feel you should be accepted. A similar experience is seen between Orthodox Jews and Reform Jews. Reform Jews devote endless pages to criticizing and badgering Orthodox Jews for not accepting their views as equally valid. Reform Jews define themselves as *reforming* Judaism to match their views of how it *should* be. Yet after succeeding they obsess over the reality that Orthodox Jews do not appreciate or accept their efforts as valid.

Orthodox Jews will respond to questions, and they will actively fight broad-sweeping determinations that affect all Jews or Jewish law when Reform Jews attempt to influence it, but they do not spend their days obsessing over how Reform Jews do not recognize or respect their view of Judaism. In the same way, trans-obsessed liberals have chosen to reform the idea of gender and obsess over the reality that average people do not accept and view their ideas as valid. Most people are perfectly happy with binary gender. Male and female is really all most need. Even with a comfort in changing one's gender it is still switching from one to the other. Hell, even when average people shrug and say *"ok, so you're bigendered or non-binary or whatever, if it works for you...cool"* they don't appreciate being repeatedly lectured on how ignorant and intolerant they are for not 100% embracing every detail of every definition created by identity-obsessed people.

The idea of infinite gender is a direct redefinition of the very concept of what gender is. These articles and the attack on Morgan just demonstrate that they will do whatever it takes to force their views to be seen. Morgan is gay-friendly under any definition, but he was turned on so quickly he could barely blink in shock. Why? Because he failed to live up to the unachievable demands of his liberal friends on this particular issue. Absolute compliance is the only acceptable option.

I am a person who has spent much of my life defining and redefining who I am. I have tweaked and adjusted my life, lifestyle, identity, religion and sexuality until I came to the conclusion of who I feel I am now. We live in a free society that allows that. But freedom and tolerance do not mean absolute acceptance and neutrality. In what appears to be the opposite, transgender activists seem bent on not just making their transition accepted, but the very idea that they exist as a separate gender altogether accepted. No longer satisfied with equal protection, insurance coverage for surgeries, workplace discrimination protection and endless TV discussions about their dignity they now demand to be viewed not only as an "other" altogether, but as an equal alternative to what is. They are not women or men; they are Trans*.

By fabricating the new slur, 'Cis', to use against those who innocently fail to submit or acknowledge their demands they bully and shame and cry in outrage until people simply get out of their way and they call this "tolerance." My personal journey through my own sense of gender is my own. It rarely affects my life, so it rarely gets mentioned. I have the experience and I can speak to it, but I do not need to be "accepted" as an "other" because of it. I am not a different kind of male. I am a person.

What liberals fails to understand in their never-ending quest to categorize every thought, feeling and action into its own protected class is that they eliminate the individual. These individuals who grew up feeling alien in their own skin are lucky enough to live in a time when they can not only embrace to their heart's content the gender expression of their choice, but they can physically transform their bodies to match. They can legally live as the other gender with absolute freedom of movement in all aspects of life. Certainly, they face struggles with relationships, their history and medical experiences, but they have the freedom to surround themselves with people who are comfortable with who they are.

A male to female transgender person can now live fully as a legal woman without anyone blinking an eye and instead of embracing this new freedom they choose to snap and lecture over every use of a pronoun or title that doesn't meet their personal view of themselves. They bicker over "transsexual, transgender, transgender*ed*, Trans, Trans* Transwoman" and on and on. They started the path to fight for the ability to embrace and transform into the opposite gender fully and now spend their time arguing over 50+ variations of "gender" and which ones they personally choose to be offended by. All the while indignant and dismissive of those "ignorant" and "intolerant" people who don't automatically embrace the world exactly as they demand it should be seen.

Coercion: How Liberals Define 'Tolerance'

March 15th, 2014

In most of the polite conversations I have with people where I can discuss the issue of Christian bakers refusing to participate in gay weddings, I have found that the majority of people rationally agree that a business should not be forced to participate in or have their brand used for a cause or event they strongly disagree with. This comes in examples such as the tattoo artist who refuses to tattoo Nazi images for a person asking, gay business owners being required to use their physical location or other services to promote or celebrate Christian events and advertisers pulling out of networks, shows or radio programs due to content concerns or religious minorities being forced to participate in activities that violate their beliefs.

Most people seem to agree that it would be wrong to require a person to participate in an event or have their brand used for a cause they do not agree with on most issues. Liberalism is fairly defined by its position that businesses with specific religious ties or owners with religious points of view should be boycotted. They spend a great deal of energy on attempting to remove speech or punish businesses they do not agree with.

The Jesuit college Fordham University Republican student group invited Ann Coulter to speak but rescinded the invitation after the university president publicly shamed them despite student membership opposing the decision. He called Coulter 'repugnant' and accused her of spreading 'hate speech'. The president responded to their decision stating: "...the leadership of the College Republicans acted quickly, took responsibility for their decisions, and expressed their regrets sincerely and eloquently."[8] It was not enough for the highest authority of the school to choose to speak out against one group of students due to his personal opinion of the speaker they chose, he had to respond to their submission to his bullying by condescendingly implying he was satisfied with their 'regret.'

This same school happily hosted a bestiality advocate, Peter Singer. "James Schall, a Jesuit and a senior government professor at Georgetown University, defended Singer's appearance at Fordham in an email to The Daily Caller. "Basically, the Church is not afraid of any idea, if it has a fair chance freely to explain its own position,"[9]

The Left has long demanded the FCC remove Rush Limbaugh from the radio with a recent demand made by both Jane Fonda and Gloria Steinem. Included is feminist, Robin Morgan, who stated in a letter "This isn't political. While we disagree with Limbaugh's politics, what's at stake is the fallout of a society tolerating toxic, hate-inciting speech. For 20 years, Limbaugh has hidden behind the First Amendment, or else claimed he's really "doing humor" or "entertainment." He is indeed constitutionally entitled to his opinions, but he is not constitutionally entitled to the people's airways."[10]

Religious therapy for Christians seeking behavioral, spiritual or psychological options for their same-sex attractions are now unable to do so due to the irrational fear the LGBT Left has for conversion or 'ex-gay' therapy in California. And of course, the LGBT Left has called for mass boycotting of the restaurant Chick Fil A for its unapologetically Christian owners who simply expressed support for traditional marriage.

Liberals use discrimination against those who hold ideologies they disagree with all the time and are incredibly proud of it. Just browsing the *Huffington Post, Salon, Slate* or *Think Progress* on any given day you will see great celebrations for any legal or social punishment against those who hold positions they believe to be wrong. Yet the various bills across the country attempting to protect religious groups from being required to participate in events they disapprove of has created a firestorm of panic throughout gay and liberal communities.

My Facebook timeline is filled with people posting articles demonizing what is being referred to as the new "Jim Crow" laws for gays. As *Star Trek* star George Takei puts it:
[11]

People seem to believe these laws are designed to allow "Gays Only" water fountains. The problem with their argument is that people could be doing that now and they aren't. Gays are not being turned away from taxis, hotels or restaurants. I can walk into any Christian bookstore in the country completely unmolested. I can go into any church or any Christian public event with my yarmulke on even and no one bats an eye.

The reason these bills even exist is because liberals insist that every person must fully embrace their view of the world without question or face the consequences. Out of dozens of non-religious cake makers, caterers, photographers and venues to choose from, liberal gays have spent the last decade marching up to specifically Christian owned businesses, announcing their sexuality and demanding they provide their services. Not a single case involved the store owner kicking the couple out or even saying "we don't serve gays here." The only thing they did was state they would not offer their services for a gay *wedding* event.

If you make cakes, take photos, own a venue or cater events you are not just selling products in a store. You are associating your brand and your business with every service you do. The future of your business relies on the experience of your customer base and how they share that experience. Christians who did not want to support, participate in or associate with an event they deeply believed to be a mockery of their very religious principles declined to do so. That's it.

Being liberals, the couples did not simply do the rational thing by taking their business elsewhere and supporting people who did not take offense to their lifestyle. Oh No. They are liberals and so they had to force the business, through courts and by law, to accept their money and provide quality service for their wedding out of pure spite. They believed they were standing up for freedom and showing everyone that their view of discrimination was unacceptable. But in reality, they used the courts to bully people to either submit to their demands or go out of business.

If you know that a business believes your incredibly special celebration to be so offensive, they refuse to bake a cake for it, why would you demand the courts force them to not only do so, but give them money for it? The whole point of choosing any service for a wedding is to pick stores that will make your day wonderful. What is supposed to happen afterwards? You make them cater your wedding, pay them and then tell everyone how tasty their cake was? Do you promote them afterwards? When people at your wedding say *'Oh! Who took these lovely photos!'* or *'This food is delicious! Who catered?'* are you going to say *'It's fabulous! It's that bakery we sued and forced to provide the food for us even though they think we're all going to hell!'* Why would you want to have symbols of the celebration of your relationship be provided by the very people who oppose it?

It makes no logical sense, but that isn't the point. They never think that far ahead. They likely sued to get national attention and never went back. The point was to publicly shame the business and then force it to close as punishment for holding the view itself.

This is the goal liberals have for anyone who opposes their point of view. They aren't satisfied with the dozens of businesses, even gay-owned businesses, that would be happy to supply services for their wedding. Unlike black people in the Jim Crow South who were simply going for dinner, riding the bus or traveling and had to face unreasonable denial everywhere they went, gays do not face this issue. The majority of businesses are happy to cater to them. They just want to punish Christians for maintaining a worldview they find offensive.

The entire point of the new proposed law is merely a reaction to the never-ending bullying tactics of the Left as described above. Conservatives want individuals to freely build their businesses and earn the trust and support of their communities through offering quality goods and services. Essentially liberals are demanding that anyone who is Christian and wishes to stay true to their principles is not allowed to own or run a business. Conservatives think that is wrong. The bills are meant to protect against that.

Again, no Christian business discriminates against gays like what was experienced by black people in the Jim Crow South. If gay people came into the store to buy a cake for a wedding the Christian business wouldn't care. It's the issue of participating and thus supporting a *gay* wedding that is the issue for them.

Zazzle.com, a website that allows users to create their own content for sale, has a policy titled *What Content is Acceptable for Designs on Zazzle?* Things that are unacceptable include: "No content that can reasonably be viewed as harassing, threatening, or otherwise harmful, No hate speech, and No content that can reasonably be viewed as discriminatory based upon race, ethnicity, national origin, sexual orientation, gender, gender identity or disability."[12]

Who decides what "Hate Speech" is exactly? Isn't a policy that may qualify my image as "hate speech" and therefore refuse service to me be discrimination against me? By liberal standards they should not be allowed to do this. But here lies the inherent conflict. Liberals want to remove what *they* view as "hate" through laws and regulations. They would not view this as discrimination if I chose to express a point of view they believe to be "hate" and I was denied.

Zazzle.com doesn't want its brand or company associated with ideas or images it is opposed to. Should that be illegal? Why is it ok for California to ban services to gays in religious counseling but it's wrong for Arizona to allow businesses to ban services to gays for weddings? Why can Zazzle block images it feels are offensive and deny its service based on that, but Christian businesses cannot deny services they find offensive?

This is not about equality; it is about liberal ideology. Liberals believe Sexual Reparative Therapy is wrong, so they ban it. Liberals believe Christians who oppose same-sex marriage should be punished so they force Christian businesses to service them by law. Liberals believe that anything they find offensive should be blocked and they believe it is perfectly moral and ethical to do so. There is no equality involved. There is only the forced application of liberal ideology onto everyone.

I have suggested that conservatives should spend a solid year demanding gay and liberal businesses service all of their events and requesting liberal TV hosts and celebrities to M.C. their events and conferences just to demonstrate the hypocrisy of it all. I'm certain Whoopi Goldberg would not find it positive to be forced by law to offer her comedic services to the Republican National Convention or be their spokesperson. Through their current demands this is the only logical outcome.

But you won't see that because conservatives, at the very basic of their nature, do not wish to enforce their views onto anyone. Liberals often cite conservative policies as attempting to do just that, but it's simply ridiculous. We oppose abortion because we do not want legalized murder of innocent people. Conservatives oppose gay marriage because they don't want a sacred and long-standing institution to be radically altered to satisfy the whims of one group of people. Nothing conservatives propose forces anyone to do anything. Everything liberals propose does force people to do things. Conservatives are mature enough to realize that if a person refuses to cater their event because they hate Republicans, they aren't worth giving money to.

If these laws passed, we would not see entire states banning gays from everyday life. There would be no "Straights Only" signs anywhere. They don't exist today; they won't exist then either. You don't even see "Christians Only" signs in Christian owned businesses or organizations. The only likely outcome, aside from the never-ending screeching of liberals, would be a few Christian owned businesses would not accept money from gay people intentionally trying to force them to participate in something they morally oppose. Liberals would never allow anything reasonable, naturally, so they would continue marching into stores, holding signs outside of them and whining on TV and blogs about how oppressed they are. But in reality, it would not be a huge issue.

The only reason it is valuable to have the law is the same reason we need a law in Florida to protect preschoolers from being expelled for eating a toaster pastry into an "L" shape which liberals think looks like a gun.[13] Without something written on paper that protects the painfully obvious common-sense position, liberals will force their idiotic ideology onto all of us without any barriers. If we could be reasonable about this, just like in my everyday conversations with people of a large variety of positions, we would recognize that the people demanding a Christian business cater their wedding are the ones being bullies. You don't have to agree with the Christian business perspective to see that. I don't think it makes a lot of sense to not sell your product or service to people who want to give you money for it, but I appreciate the idea that some people attach moral ethics to how they run business. Aren't liberals constantly complaining about businesses taking actions without regards to moral principles all the time "just for the money?"

Gays need to grow up and stop whining every time they discover someone doesn't like them, or really, imagine this to be the case. The law does not ban gay wedding services. It does not state that businesses must discriminate. It does not do anything but protect a minority from being bullied into either giving up their principles or going out of business. This is a case where the concept overrides the logic and reality. People *think* it's just like Jim Crow laws, so they react as though they are and refuse to listen to any other position. They ignore the consequences of their actions and will likely sing songs of victory when the public pressure forces these laws to be shut down.

In the end Christians, will be the only ones discriminated against as they will be forced to choose either to participate and support something they are morally opposed to, or be silenced and forced out of business for not complying. We are witnessing true oppression of thought celebrated by the champions of "equality" and "tolerance.

The Cake is a Lie

March 20th, 2014

IN AN ARTICLE TITLED, *Blue State Blues: The Gay Intolerance Act of 2014*, writer Joel Pollack discusses his observations into liberal intolerance: "Though Gov. Jan Brewer's decision was probably justified, what the entire episode demonstrated is that gay intolerance enjoys a certain degree of legal and political protection. Again, this is not unusual: it is the kind of deference our society often shows towards minority groups. Filmmaker Spike Lee's rant this week against the white people gentrifying Harlem (hello, Bill Clinton) would have been unthinkable had the races been reversed."

In my own community, there is widespread, if muted, anti-Christian intolerance that is considered not just acceptable but fashionable. It forms the basis of much of Sarah Silverman's comedy schtick, for example. It is also a major reason why so many American Jews vote Democrat: they are afraid of evangelicals. One result: There is no one more philo-Semitic in U.S. politics than Sarah Palin, and yet liberal Jews still recoil in horror."[14]

I have talked about the idea of coercion as a means to obtain an idea of "equality" or "justice." liberals often believe that ends justify the means when it comes to a concept like "Civil Rights" and they refuse to acknowledge the consequences such actions can cause. They are never satisfied with rational solutions and instead favor more aggressive and continuous action believing the fight must continue otherwise all their work will fall apart. Liberals have a basic belief that humanity is slanted towards evil, and it is necessary to maintain strict control.

What other reason could explain the tidal wave of demands that a new era of segregation will befall us if a single law in a single state were not defeated? Gays are not being ushered out of restaurants or being sent to the back of buses. No business in America, regardless of religious affiliation, is actively or even passively discriminating against any group of people, especially gay people. Gays can move freely and as openly as they choose in all walks of life without even a single disapproving glare from those around them. Yet if you only saw the news for the last year or so you would think we were being sprayed with water hoses as we marched down the streets trying to obtain equal voting rights.

The irony is that if Arizona law SB 1062 had not made news and had continued on in relative obscurity, gays in the state would never have noticed. The only experience they would have had would have been the sad disappointment that their bully tactics did not hit as hard in court any longer. The new law, already passed btw, amended a previous law that already gave protections to religious groups. Essentially the new law amended the old one to be more specific and broaden the target group. It allowed religious businesses. organizations, venues and individuals within businesses to have a defense platform if they chose to refrain from participating in an activity or event that violated their beliefs and were sued for doing so.

If, say, Susie Christian decided to exercise her beliefs by kicking out gay couples from her diner and one couple sued, she would not be protected because the gay couple eating in her restaurant did not "substantially burden" her practice of religion. But if she owned a photography business and she were asked to attend a same-sex wedding and offer her photography services and declined, she could argue that participating in the event, associating her brand with the event and actively supporting the event through her work substantially affected her religious practice and she could have protection from the lawsuit. That really was the extent of the bill.

People argued that it broadened the options and therefore could invite discrimination. The primary liberal alarm was that the law would create an environment where gays and lesbians were openly mistreated by businesses in public and would bring us back to the Jim Crow South era of discrimination. The part that was missed, however, if that all of those things could already be happening right now. Anti-discrimination laws just give people the ability to sue a business for discriminating against them. It becomes in the interest of the business to not discriminate against the various protected classes. Businesses today could be aggressively discriminating against gays all over the place with or without a religious protection law, but they aren't.

The reality is that no business wants to invite negative publicity, lose customers or really, discriminate against anybody. Even the cases that sparked this debate didn't involve discrimination against gays directly. They could have purchased cakes in the store, hired the cater for a birthday party or used the venue for a rock concert. No one was telling gay people they weren't allowed on the premises. The issue was involvement in gay weddings and whether or not Christian business owners wished to participate or associate themselves and their services.

Gay marriage has been a dramatic dividing issue in our country and Christians in particular have felt it as the last battle ground in their fight for traditional values. Gay groups didn't obtain enough votes or political influence to legally usher in new standards for marriage in the states to include theirs so they sued and sued until they forced their will. Christians, Conservatives and other religious groups demanded their voices be heard and gays and liberals silenced them. In the progressive style of doing things, gays obtained 99% of the market on thought in the public arena but could not tolerate the remaining 1% of businesses, churches and other religious organizations who would not bend to their will, so they sued them.

Back when I was active in the gay liberal world, we often intentionally marched into stores and demanded some special accommodation just to see if we would be refused. I badgered bookstore managers as to the location of the "gay section" as being in the back of the store, the gay magazines on the bottom shelf and even that there was a "gay" section at all for example. I even made my store manager reach out to the head office of a bookstore I worked at to explain why the store carried a 'gay and lesbian fiction' section. All gay marriage lawsuits begin with a gay couple going to the courthouse, requesting a marriage license, being denied and then suing for discrimination. With dozens of bakeries, catering services and photographers to choose from, there is no logical reason to target a Christian owned business. This isn't about logic; however, it is about domination.

From an article titled: *Anti-Gay Christian Leader Whines About How Gay Couples Want Equal Treatment at Christian-Owned Businesses*, "In short, all Smith can find are instances where gay couples were hoping to be treated the same way straight couples are. And he's taking the side of Christians who wanted to delegate the gay couples to second-class status because of their sexual orientation. You expect to see that sort of bigotry within the walls of a church — and the actions would be legal in a church setting — but these states have made clear that public businesses don't get to deny their services to people who are black or Muslim or atheist or female or handicapped — or gay. Your "conscience" be damned. Just as you can't hang a "No Jews Allowed" sign in front of your public floral business, you can't tell gay couples you're not going to bake a cake for their ceremony when you offer the same services to everybody else."[15]

Here is the point of view from one such baker, Sweet Cakes, sued for discrimination about their experience: "It started on Jan. 17 when a mother and daughter showed up at

Sweet Cakes by Melissa looking for the perfect wedding cake. "My first question is what's the wedding date," said owner Aaron Klein. "My next question is bride and groom's name ... the girl giggled a little bit and said it's two brides." Klein apologized to the women and told them he and his wife do not make cakes for same-sex marriages. Klein said the women were disgusted and walked out. "I believe that marriage is a religious institution ordained by God," said Klein. "A man should leave his mother and father and cling to his wife ... that to me is the beginning of marriage." I apologized for wasting their time and said we don't do same-sex marriages. honestly did not mean to hurt anybody, didn't mean to make anybody upset, (it's) just something I believe in very strongly."[16]

The argument in the first quote comes from a standpoint that putting up a "No Jews Allowed" sign and refusing to make a cake for a gay wedding are the same thing. Liberal thinking often lumps concepts together to strengthen a weaker argument with a stronger one even if they aren't fully connected. A more reasonable comparison would be if the writer in the first quote were asked to write an article for a Christian magazine defending traditional marriage and he declined.

Offering your service is direct association. People get fussy about extreme comparisons, but most would understand that kicking out known KKK members from your restaurant is different than refusing to allow them to rent your restaurant out for meetings every other Tuesday. The first is passing judgment on a person and the second is refusing to associate yourself with that person or their cause.

While gay and liberal arguments are often about equal treatment, they ignore the relevant point of view that forcing someone to support something they oppose is in itself wrong. Somewhere along the maddening few days of Facebook and twitter arguing I found absurdity in the whole thing. In one particular group discussion, it dawned on us that the entire debacle has started because a gay couple asked for a cake, and they were told no. "Cake Equality!" and "Equal Access to Cake!" seemed like hilarious ways to approach this concept. While there are certainly larger concepts around this, in the end it was all about the damn cake.

Are we so comfortable in our world that national outrage can be over a business refusing to bake a cake? This was never a threat to gay freedom or even our national obsession with equality at all costs. This was about stamping out the last bits of opposition to the current liberal mindset on homosexuality and the role gay people play in our society. If we honestly just wanted to be treated like everyone else, we would not be cornering small bakeries and driving them out of business because they did not support our wedding.

From 'We Shall Overcome' to 'Bake Me a Cake!'

March 25th, 2014

HAVE WE REALLY COME so far in our struggle for equality that we now bicker over who will bake a cake for whom and why? Liberal gays have a baked-in belief that Christians are hiding behind every corner just waiting to oppress them. Read any article on any liberal website and you will see nothing but seething hatred for the "right" and Christians. Even though Christians, in large, rarely speak above a polite hush on the topic and merely quote the Bible when discussing homosexuality, liberal gays obsess over even the tiniest hint that they are not fully, 100%, accepted in all areas of life. Ironic for a group that has always prided itself on being counter-culture.

In *The United State of Tara,* a Showtime series about a woman with multiple personalities, we see a great example. One episode revolves around the son, Marshall dealing with how gay he wants to be. His friend, Lionel, represents the loud activist gay in the show. The high school has an event every year in which students can purchase a red, pink or yellow carnation and give it to the person they love, like or are just friends with. Lionel decides this discriminates against gays and demands a purple carnation be introduced to include the various degrees of queer students on campus. The school, reasonably, declines and tells him to simply use the color code the other students use as they are not gender specific and have nothing to do with sexual orientation. The episode ends with the father, Max and Marshall bringing purple-dyed carnations to the school anyway to hand out in an act of rebellion.

When I watched this, it perfectly illustrated the gay movement of recent years for me. We already have just about everything in exact equal proportion to everybody else. Most gays individually experience absolutely nothing different than their straight counterparts. Gay people are only recognized as being gay if they verbally announce it, dress or behave in a socially recognized way or are with a partner. People do not stop and stare, pointing in disgust, when they see one of us. Most people know someone who is gay very well and even those who hold strong religious beliefs that oppose homosexuality interact with gay people on a regular basis. People who insist they are being harassed or tormented by anti-gay bullying in everyday life are simply lying or imagining it. I have gone years, a full decade now, without even a hint of anything negative directed at me for my sexuality and I live in rural West Virginia.

The fact that gay people are physically attacked or harassed in instances around the country does not equal a wide-spread hatred of gay people. Most negative associations with gay people are towards the collective group rather than the individual. This has not been true for previous generations of oppressed minorities. Simply put: people may disagree with same-sex marriage, but they are perfectly polite and comfortable with the gay people they know in real life.

The TV series later includes an episode where Marshall asks his now boyfriend Lionel to attend his aunt's wedding to which Lionel protests because gay marriage isn't widely accepted or legal throughout the country. He finally agrees under further protest until he meets Marshall's sister's new boyfriend who reveals he is a libertarian (he supports Ron Paul) and does not support gay marriage (a clear example of how liberals don't grasp other points of view) to which he storms off in righteous indignation. The libertarian is a handsome, self-made wealthy 27-year-old offering the world to the 17 year old sister Kate but she chooses to dismiss him entirely from her life after first gasping in bewildered shock when learning he did not vote for Obama followed by a hushed *"are...are you a Republican?"* and then later expressing her disgust that he does not think her brother deserves a wedding. The very existence of a different point of view is enough to set off liberal alarms and protest.

The Arizona law, SB1062, debacle illustrates exactly how the left views and responds to opposing positions. By demanding Christian businesses provide services for gay weddings and suing when they were denied, gay liberals reveal their true intentions. They have no interest in equality, free speech, freedom of religion or association or anything else most of us take for granted. They simply want total domination for their point of view. They legitimately believe it is superior and the only true and righteous way and they will do anything to stamp out opposition.

The reoccurring question in this argument has been over equating the Civil Rights movement with the Gay Rights movement. Liberals tend to assert they are identical while conservatives tend to separate the two from each other. Most policies that "discriminate" against gays have absolutely nothing to do with gay people at all. While Jim Crow laws were specifically to separate black people *from* white people, laws and policies gays fight over are not designed to separate gay people from straight people.

For example: If a gym offers spouse or family discounts and a gay couple apply for it and are denied, this is not discrimination against gay people. Any combination of unmarried individuals or individuals without children would be denied the discount. The owners did not set up the policy to intentionally prevent gays from joining their gym. They simply made what is a widely practiced and pretty standard-issue policy that makes reasonable sense in our society. The gym is more accurately discriminating against single people since it is essentially giving preference to those who are married or have children.

The gym could simply state that everyone pays one amount, and a husband and wife would individually pay that amount. But being a business, the gym wants to encourage more customers and so offers levels of discounts. It is logical to give a discounted rate for two people who are married while requiring two non-married people to pay separate rates.

Gay people view this as a personal attack on them since they can never qualify for the discount. They view it as unfair that their relationship is not being recognized as equal to the married couples who get the discount. From a perfectly objective point of view, they are actually two singles asking for the married rate. Any two singles asking for the married rate would be equally denied, but because this particular couple happen to be gay it is deemed anti-gay discrimination. This is true with insurance, hospital visits, adoption and so on. Each policy is designed for a married couple and gays interpret denial of the service as discrimination when really, it's just an eligibility issue.

The valid argument is whether or not a business should widen its definitions to include more kinds of couples. The invalid argument is to demand that failing to do so is intentional discrimination. If a same-sex couple were legally married in a state that recognizes said marriage, applies for the married discount and denied because the gym does not support gay relationships – then it can be viewed as anti-gay discrimination.

All "anti-gay" laws that exist are actually laws that specifically support a married couple as distinct from two single people. Anti-Gay laws are more accurately viewed as pro-marriage laws since all single individuals are denied the benefit. In reality gays are not special in this case. There are cases to be made around all kinds of human couplings and families and many businesses adjust their policies to match their clientele. A good example would be my own gym membership. My gym offers a "spouse" discount when a spouse is added to the account. I asked, without knowing any of the policies, if I could add a friend to my account and just pay his monthly fee. I didn't ask for a discount at all. The lady smiled and said, *"Well I will just add him as your "spouse" and you can get the discounted rate."* He and I are not in a relationship. He is a friend pure and simple, and I never indicated otherwise.

When allowed freedom, a business owner is likely to make decisions that both please his customers and earn him more money. It makes business sense to add a same-sex partner at a discount since you now have a larger payment than the single by himself and you don't risk losing his payment if he leaves. If a gym chooses to maintain a non-flexible policy, there are dozens of other gyms to go to.

A couple I am friends with lived together for years before marrying. They were treated as singles the entire time. They and I had actual equal treatment under the law. She did not get access to his work benefits until after they were married. Had he and I lived together, and we were dating, his work would have denied me access as well. But calling it an "anti-gay" policy would simply be incorrect.

Sodomy laws are often invoked to argue how Christians attempted to legally oppress gays in the past. But again, the laws applied to anyone engaging in the activities. They were not intended to simply punish gay men but were an attempt to conform sexuality under the religious umbrella of marriage. By default, gay men would violate the law, but the law was not intended for gay men.

From an article on Sodomy Laws from *The Nation: We Colonials: Sodomy Laws in America*

"Take the scholarship on the colonial era, with which Eskridge begins his account. During the 1600s, the American colonies adopted sodomy (or "buggery") laws that prohibited bestiality as well as anal sex between either a man and a woman or between two men. (New Haven Colony was rare in including sexual acts between women as part of its sodomy prohibition.) Punishment–which included death–was draconian, but the laws were very rarely enforced. Historians know of less than ten executions for sodomy throughout the seventeenth century. Of those few, almost all involved assault or sex with animals.

These laws were not directed in any particular way toward homosexuality. Indeed, they couldn't be–the idea that there was a type of person who was a homosexual didn't even emerge until the late nineteenth century, a result of urbanization, industrialization and the development of medical/sexological discourse. But while these laws weren't about discouraging homosexuality per se, their architects sought to regulate sexual behavior more generally by steering sexuality toward procreative marriage; protecting women, children and weaker men from assault; and maintaining public order and decency."[17]

It wasn't until the Sexual Revolution that a backlash of Morality Police hit and began enforcing sodomy laws specifically in terms of arresting homosexuals. Homosexuality was considered a mental illness to which one could be institutionalized. Think of the many ways we manipulate laws to add up to a larger offense today. In any arrest a person is usually charged with multiple offenses in the hopes that one will stick. Sometimes offenses are merely the excuse to arrest in the first place.

Similar to the progressive anti-alcohol laws as a way to conform society, sexual deviancy laws were meant to keep the average person in a socially accepted framework. Adultery, prostitution, sodomy etc. were all the exact same concept. They went against the institution of marriage. The first gay pride parades, marches and demonstrations were so over-the-top with men and women nearly naked and dressed in the most obscene and flamboyant ways largely to protest the idea of these morality laws which could intimidate individuals but not an entire population. Imagine today seeing a parade of people engaging in the most over-the-top drug usage possible as a demonstration that the police cannot get them all. Same concept.

Over time the parades have become more symbolic; at the time, they were actively breaking the law in protest. They weren't demonstrating against anti-gay laws. They were protesting all gender-conforming laws and social demands. Women were topless, men openly kissing or dressed as women etc. And this really brings me to my point. Like women, black people and other minorities who risked being thrown in jail for breaking discriminatory laws, gays did the same thing when the law was used against them even though it was never intended for them at all.

Over time the results of that struggle have created a society where gays can move freely unmolested and without fear. In fact, when stories emerge of actual mistreatment of a person for their sexuality, as with the gay waitress who reported having an anti-gay message scrawled on her receipt (which turned out to be hoax), the media explodes in outrage.[18] Even people on the right who do not agree with homosexuality do not attack the individual and demand they deserve the mistreatment. Instead, nearly every person agrees no one should be mistreated at all.

I recognize that I can be safely myself in public and in all areas of life because of the struggle of those who came before me and fought true oppression. Men who realized they had same-sex attractions went to bars that were known to be places where similar men went. Police raided these places out of actual prejudice and bigotry. Men and women who were doing nothing more than connecting with one another in secret were targeted. Today people simply no longer experience this.

But like the never-ending demands of racism and sexism that are also more rare than real, gay liberals still feel the need to declare oppression. This is what happens when a group defines itself by those who hate them. Without hatred towards them there is nothing to hold them together. Gay people no longer need to congregate in cities to escape rural danger. We no longer need our own bookstores to fill the gap in mainstream bookstores. TV shows have more gay characters in them than you find in real life. Individual gay people simply go about their lives, date and coexist freely with their straight friends.

Yet without the constant alarm from the left, the gay world would find itself fairly obsolete. We no longer, for example, need a NAACP, but do you think those who obtain social status, fame or money from that are going to give it up? To accept social peace and integrate naturally into the whole is not betraying the struggles of the past. It should be a celebration of them. We're done guys! If allowed, the vast majority of businesses and states would adjust their policies to include same-sex couples on their own. They have been for a while now. I challenge you to find a large business, or even a small one, that actively avoids adding same-sex coverage to their benefits. The last real areas are over how marriage will be viewed state to state and federally as well as adoption. That's really it.

Adoption, like marriage, it merely a state-approved list of eligibility requirements. Adoption was taken over by the state and is regulated by it and has the absolute full encyclopedia of liberal ideas on child-rearing. To adopt a child is a mind-boggling process of hoops you'd never dream of in a rational world. While there are certainly religious groups who deem a gay couple as harmful to children, most states are more concerned with fulfilling their endless list of parenting permits than they are the number of genders involved.

The reality is that we have it pretty good. Liberals cry about how evil and oppressive our country is, I think, because if people ever got the chance to listen to their views without the aid of irrelevant but emotional barriers no one would let them anywhere near a position of authority. Demanding that this or that group is discriminated against invokes the natural compassion most people have and disguises the intention behind it. Liberals, I think, absolutely believe themselves. I went through class after class describing the millions of teeny tiny ways people can experience sexism and racism which make most average people raise an eyebrow or roll their eyes. We have come from "We Shall Overcome" to "Bake Me a Cake!" as our cry for freedom. Access to wedding cake is the defining civil rights issue of our time. We cannot obtain the level of maturity required to realize that if a bakery feels it violates their freedom of religion to bake you a cake for your wedding that maybe you should take your business elsewhere?

Our social oppression went from targeting people for thinking or behaving or simply being what we do not like and punishing them to, well exactly the same thing. Police raiding a gay bar to enforce a law against men dressing as women as a way to declare social intolerance for that behavior and attempt to prevent it from spreading and suing a business for holding a belief we think is wrong and refusing to participate in an activity we think is beautiful and punishing them for it is the exact same thing.

When gay people simply wanted to exist without causing harm to anyone in their own place in the world and were hunted down for it, it was wrong. When Christians want the same thing and we do the same thing to them, it's still wrong. Why did it matter so much that a handful of men were dressing up as women in a bar at the edge of town? Why does it matter so much now that a handful of religious people want to remain separate from mainstream views and run their businesses in peace? What liberals always fail to understand is that they are controlled by the Progressive belief that you can enforce morality through force. What they further fail to realize is that by giving this belief legal authority, they never know when they will once again find themselves the victim of it.

Bullying Our Way Through

March 27th, 2014

THE TENNESSEE "RELIGIOUS VIEWPOINTS Antidiscrimination Act" is suddenly receiving the not-exactly-true treatment from liberal sources as other religious freedom bills have. In all cases, the people outraged the most apparently haven't actually read it. In breathless panic gays and liberals around the country are screaming that, as Back2Stonewall puts it: *Tennessee Passes Bill Allowing The Bullying of LGBT Students in the Name of 'Religious Freedom.'*"

The Tennessee "Religious Viewpoints Antidiscrimination Act" allows students to use religion in any manner they choose and protects their use of religion. The ACLU warns that the bill, SB 1793/HB 1547, "crosses the line from protecting religious freedom into creating systematic imposition of some students' personal religious viewpoints on other students." The entire article only manages to assume that in some worst case scenario Christian students could express their religious views to the detriment of gay students.

Let's start with what the bill actually states. "This bill prohibits an LEA from discriminating against a student based on a religious viewpoint expressed by the student on an otherwise permissible subject. This bill requires an LEA to treat a student's voluntary expression of a religious viewpoint, if any, on an otherwise permissible subject in the same manner the LEA treats a student's voluntary expression of a secular or other viewpoint on an otherwise permissible subject."[19]

It goes on to detail out specifics such as: "This bill specifies that a student may express beliefs about religion in homework, artwork, and other written and oral assignments free from discrimination based on the religious content of their submissions. A student would not be penalized or rewarded on account of the religious content of the student's work." and clarifies that students can organize social groups with religious purposes.

This is what everyone is all enraged over. According to the above Back2Stonewall article: "An evangelical student, or example, could preach the gospel during a science class, or "witness" during English. Attacks on LGBT people and same-sex marriage are automatically protected under this bill, offering anti-gay students a state-sposored license to bully. And of course, a student could claim they worship Satan and subject their classmates to that "religious viewpoint" as well."[20]

'Attacks' and 'Bullying' seem to now cover expressing personal opinions gay liberals do not agree with. How is expressing a viewpoint opposing same-sex marriage any more or less of an attack on gay students than expressing a viewpoint supporting same-sex marriage is on a Christian student? Isn't the point of education to widen your point of view with new and different information so that you can develop your own opinion on any given subject?

If there is only one correct answer, then there is no development. Every question can be viewed in different ways with different angles. Religious points of view are not excluded from that development. It is not "bullying" to hear a point of view you disagree with.

The bill does not prevent students from expressing anti-religious points of view so what is stopping gay or liberal students from expressing their counterviews? Are only liberal gay students allowed to have a vocal opinion on any given subject?

To be more accurate this bill does not deal with Christians at all as it covers all religious individuals. No one seems too concerned that a Muslim or a Jew might express religious viewpoints that may be deemed unacceptable. The bill does not override anti-bullying policies or allow physical violence. If one read's the bill it clearly indicates that it protects, essentially, freedom of speech on "otherwise permissible subjects."

To demand that there is only a single correct way to view any educational topic is a religious view in of itself. Students use all manner of experience to express opinions, opposition or questions to topics presented in school and religious experience cannot be excluded from that.

Liberal gays seem both offended and threatened by the very existence of an opposition point of view. I am a gay person and the reality that many people of many faiths view me as a sinful person has absolutely no impact on my life. Attempting to force the point of view that being gay is a normal and natural experience through actual bullying by coercing students to accept it without any option to dissent is equally as oppressive as religiously mandating the opposite.

There is a clear bigotry that has grown in our community against specifically Christians, and it is expressed in overreactions to the very knowledge that they do not agree with us. We demand they are attacking us when they merely state their opinion based on their own religious perspective and yet we feel compelled to demand they accept ours.

The bills here and in Arizona were created in response to this. It is absurd to require special legislation to allow students the freedom to express their religious ideas and opinions in schoolwork, yet we have to do so. This in no way negatively affects gay students unless we are asserting that hearing any dissent is harmful.

We also need to embrace the virtues of honesty and accurate interpretations. We too often fly off the handle at any internet story or posting that *sounds like* 'Christians are discriminating against us!' and we refuse to listen to any factual clarification afterwards. We are so engrained in actual bigotry that new information is irrelevant to us.

The quoted story is a lie and yet thousands like it are circulated as an alarm and embraced by thousands more who will never even care to dig any deeper. They assume Christians want to oppress us so it must be true. We have become the close-minded, hate-filled bigots we have fought against for so long.

Reason and rationality would tell us that if Tennessee must pass this kind of a law, then we are all in trouble. The very nature of our freedom to associate and our freedom of speech and religious expression are dissolving. Liberal gays may think this is a good thing when it impacts their ideological foes, but they fail to recognize they are cutting the ropes to the bridge they are standing on too.

By aggressively limiting 'hurt feelings' speech we endanger our own speech. Real and honest speculation is not that Evangelicals will take over a science class and make all the gay kids cry with their quoting of the bible. Real projection into the future tells us that if we can legally suppress the expression, we find offensive today it only takes a power-shift to become oppressed ourselves in the future.

Who cares if a Christian kid thinks or says that homosexuality is a sin? Are we so thin-skinned that we cannot rebuff that? Are our arguments so shaky and frail that they cannot withstand a Bible quotation? Is our version of equality and freedom a world where no one can disagree with us?

We must learn to be strong enough to fight our own battles rather than sue and legislate opposition out of existence. We should be brave enough to withstand dissent without it crushing our entire worldview. We must be the leaders of free thought and expression by not only allowing but encouraging everyone to feel safe and secure in how they feel and think openly.

The only way to win over a person's mind is to first respect their point of view. All we are doing now is bullying people who we dare question our position and celebrate in victory when they are sufficiently silenced into oblivion.

The Last Stage of Humanity: A Pro-Life Argument

April 3rd, 2014

BEING PRO-LIFE SEEMS SO natural to me that I genuinely struggle sometimes to understand why people are Pro-Choice. I used to be Pro-Choice, but that was before I knew the details. But in my debating online I have come to understand that the arguments almost always miss the point. For me Pro-Life is about the importance of human equality. I don't mean this the way progressives do which typically involves equal outcome and a focus on the differences involved in humanity rather than the underlying equality of human life.

For me all people are created equally, and I feel that is the very base of our morality. All people have the exact same *value*. What they choose to do with their lives and the consequences of their actions vary later on, but we are each born equal in value. Without this basic understanding, you will always have the horrors of oppression, genocide, slavery and every other consequence of placing differing values on differing groups of people.

An interesting note here is that Pro-Choice advocates often stop the conversation here and demand that you must then oppose the death penalty, war and embrace social equality otherwise you are a hypocrite. Ironically since they support all of those things by the base of their argument you would think they'd see their own hypocrisy in supporting abortion. If you can see the difference between an innocent infant and a guilty murderer, then you can clearly understand how supporting the death penalty and being Pro-Life are mutually exclusive.

To compare human value at birth with the consequences of mass-murdering others you would have to equate the death penalty with randomly executing individuals based solely on the personal choice of another human being without a crime being committed. We can debate the relative morality around when it is and when it is not okay to take human life under broad concepts like the judicial system or in war, but it isn't truly relevant to the termination of human life purely on the decision that said life is inconvenient to another person.

This is why medical issues related to the safety of the mother are also irrelevant to the discussion of abortion. In every discussion, I am involuntarily forced into a corner with the demand to choose between the mother or the baby in an unlikely and completely hypothetical situation. For some reason the answer that the decision is literally impossible due to both lives being equal in value is simply not accepted. Somehow being opposed to elective abortion makes me King Solomon.

When asked if in a medical emergency if I had to choose between the mother or the baby, I always attempt to reason with an equally impossible scenario of being solely responsible for rescuing either a mother or her baby from a burning car. Most people cannot answer that one either. It makes sense to somberly state that in a medical emergency it is best to end the baby's life to save the mother, but no one seems to agree that allowing the baby to burn in the car is the best choice.

The fact that the mother is an adult, can make more babies and is somehow more valuable to society is little comfort in the burning car scenario. The "health of the mother" issue is tricky because there is no clear-cut scenario involved. Obviously, the doctors will attempt to save both the mother and the baby. If the baby is too undeveloped to survive on its own outside of the womb and there is a medical complication that endangers the life of the mother, then it is a lack of medical advancement, not elective abortion.

The baby is not going to survive if the mother dies, and our medical technology is not advanced enough to save it. If the baby is able to survive on its own outside the womb, then every effort will be made to remove the baby safely and stabilize the mother.

I am sure there are many medical emergencies which can complicate this, but the primary goal is to save both lives if possible. There is no choice to cut open the mother, take the baby out and let her bleed to death while the doctors walk away. There is no scenario where the only option is to end the mother's life in order to save the baby's. The baby must be removed from the mother's body due to the emergency and so there is no reason to terminate it first. I cannot imagine a scenario where the doctor tells the mother she must choose to terminate her baby right this minute or face an untimely death herself.

The problem is that liberals take an obvious situation that places the mother in danger and broaden it to "risks." If a woman decides she is "at risk" for a complication which may or may not occur, she should be able to terminate the pregnancy. They file this under the same category as an emergency. If the mother discovers her pregnancy will be life threatening it is obviously going to put the baby in danger as well and we go right back to my original point. If you question why I think liberals would unnecessarily broaden the definition to absurd levels, please see children bringing a gun to school with the intent to kill their classmates and children who point their finger in the shape of a gun at recess and the liberal response.

Rape is also brought up in discussions as though it alone determines the fate of the entire topic. Just as most would agree there is a difference between stabbing a man trying to rape you and stabbing a man who is dating you but cheated, there is a difference between elective abortion and abortion related to rape. My personal stance is that the value of the baby does not change.

Terminating a baby because it was conceived through rape is still subjectively ending the life of an innocent person for the psychological comfort of the mother. Imagine if the mother found out her two-year-old was the product of a rape she suppressed and remembered through therapy and then decided to kill it in order to ease her psychological pain.

I am a rape survivor, and I cannot imagine how difficult it would be to become pregnant from a rape. But I personally do not think it justifies an abortion. Oddly feminism is very clear on the irrelevancy of the father or his genetic influence in terms of single mothers except in this one case. In all seriousness, though, I think common sense and compassion are widely held for this scenario. No mean man in a suit is angrily pointing at a rape victim and demanding she give birth and raise the child or go to prison. Similar to self- defense, even though killing another person is still wrong we understand that the extreme situation makes for an extreme exception.

I would also point out that abortion for a rape victim is not all-inclusive. If the rape victim chooses to wait until her sixth month or later, she cannot have an abortion. The reason this particular argument tactic infuriates me is because it is only used as a way to silence opposition to the topic by shaming. Sensible procedures would give the option to take a pill to prevent pregnancy from occurring when reported and honest compassion can allow an actual abortion if pregnancy is discovered a few weeks later.

My primary concern is elective abortion. The human equality point of view is most relevant here. If you walked up to a woman holding her three hour-old baby, took it and crushed its skull you would go to prison for the rest of your life. No one would defend such an action. It boggles my mind that three hours earlier the baby is considered a lifeless lump of flesh or at best "just a fetus" with no rights or humanity.

But let's say we all agree that late-term abortions are wrong. Where do we go from there? If eight months is too late, is six months also too late? What about five months? If we determine it by viability, then wouldn't that change with medical advancements? What is the difference between a 25-week-old baby and a 20-week-old baby?

The earlier you go into the pregnancy doesn't change the baby itself, it just shows a different development stage. From the moment of conception, the baby is a unique human being and begins rapidly developing. It's not a religious or science fiction concept. The DNA doesn't change from some amorphous nothing into a unique person at exactly 25 weeks. Literally from conception it is a unique human being and begins the long process of development into a full-grown human.

To argue that a two-week-old fetus is less valuable than a 25-week-old fetus which is less valuable than a day-old baby is to argue that a two-year-old is less valuable than a five-year-old. Imagine your viability as a human being worthy of living being determined on the number of years you have achieved. At 12 you are "just a pre-teen" and therefore can be killed if you become a burden, but at 13 you become a teenager and can work for the family, so you are spared? Its lunacy.

Also, even though the development of an infant into a child into a teenager and so on displays dramatic physical, emotional and intellectual changes, we do not assert that an adult was never a teenager or a child. A person remains the same person from the day they are born until the day they die. So why is it so foreign to understand that this extends before birth?

We do not look at poor people and determine that a culling of their children is required to prevent further strain on the adults. We do not look at sick people and murder the ones whose families "choose" to do so. Why do we not only view it as acceptable but as the pinnacle of women's rights to do just that with pregnancy?

Can you imagine if people argued it would be best for society if we killed a 1/3rd of the poor population to ease strain on the overall economy? Amazingly, the left routinely argues just this very concept. In a *Huffington Post* article titled, *Abortion Poverty Study Finds Link Between Lack Of Access And Income*, argues, "When a woman is denied the abortion she wants, she is statistically more likely to wind up unemployed, on public assistance, and below the poverty line,"[21] lead researcher Dr. Diana Greene Foster explained, "Another conclusion we could draw is that denying women abortions places more burden on the state because of these new mothers' increased reliance on public assistance programs."[22]

Pro-Life advocates often use slavery as a relevant point towards the discussion and the reason is because it is the last time in our modern history where we placed an inherent value on the life of a person. White people valued black people less and therefore could sell them, own them and determine the path of their entire lives. By determining that a person's inherent value is dependent on their current stage of development is equally as horrendous and illogical.

When a woman becomes pregnant it is no longer an issue of what she wants as an individual because there are now two individuals involved. The baby's life is equal in value to the mother's life. She should have no more determination over what is done with that life than she would with mine. I cannot terminate inconvenient people around me, it makes no sense that a woman can terminate her baby for being inconvenient to her.

President Obama stated on the 41st Anniversary to Roe V Wade: "We reaffirm our steadfast commitment to protecting a woman's access to safe, affordable health care and her constitutional right to privacy, including the right to reproductive freedom," he continued. "And we resolve to reduce the number of unintended pregnancies, support maternal and child health, and continue to build safe and healthy communities for all our children. Because this is a country where everyone deserves the same freedom and opportunities to fulfill their dreams."[23]

This assumes that if a woman becomes pregnant she cannot "fulfill her dreams" and if she gets an abortion she will be able to do so. But again, if she decides five years after having the baby that she wants to now "fulfill her dreams" we do not get weepy-eyed and applaud her for dropping her child off at the mall and dancing away towards her bliss. It is also ironic that "everyone deserves the same freedom and opportunities to fulfill their dreams" except those who are currently developing in their mother's womb.

Women have absolute "reproductive freedom" in our country. Women are not lined up at the DMV for their yearly pregnancy requirement and unlike China, we do not limit how many children a woman can have. A woman can have a child with a different father every year if she chooses. She can purchase sperm and artificially impregnate herself. She can carry the baby of another couple for them.

She can sell her eggs. She can have her eggs removed and stored for later use. She can choose to never have a child. She can be a lesbian, be a nun, or have exclusively anal sex if she wants. Contraception is widely available in many forms for both her and her male partner. That pretty much defines "reproductive freedom."

Privacy has nothing to do with murder. She would not have the right to privacy to suffocate her newborn baby for example. Women have the exact same access to "affordable" healthcare as men do. Men are not seated ahead of women in hospitals across the nation with preferred treatment. Women are not denied treatment that men can readily access.

The issue is deciding that a person, in this case a woman, can intentionally end the life of another person solely based on her personal preference. It would be easier for a woman to murder her husband than divorce him, in order to "fulfill her dreams" but we certainly don't see that as a viable option. We don't celebrate men who wish to "fulfill their dreams" by abandoning the woman they impregnated either. The only situation in which it is acceptable to murder another person solely for your own convenience is abortion.

The other side of the argument

The physical experience of a woman who goes through pregnancy is extreme. It is not a light thing to go through and birth is exceptionally difficult. No one is underplaying this role. Pro-Choice advocates often demand that a woman is being "forced" to complete her pregnancy even if she doesn't want the changes to happen to her body or go through the risk and difficulty of giving birth.

These are valid concerns. Again, a woman in America is not being held down by state police and impregnated. She has absolute choice in the matter. The larger issue is the liberal obsession with consequence-free sex.

Suffice it to say, no organized group is demanding that women have even a social obligation to become pregnant. If "reproductive freedom" is the goal, then women's groups should be funding medical research to harness the mechanism of pregnancy to make it more accessible. We have the social freedoms already, both men and women should have the ability to activate their reproductive capabilities at will. We have great advances in contraception, but we could always find more ways for a woman to simply turn off or on her ability to become pregnant. The solution should not be to "hope for the best" and end the lives of innocent people when things go wrong.

I have absolutely no interest in directing anyone's personal life choices. The argument that the government should stay out of a woman's body are misleading, just as President Obama's implication that privacy is involved. Intentionally ending the life of another person is murder. Murder involves the rights of two people and therefore is not a "personal medical decision" or a privacy issue.

My concern is for the equally valuable life helplessly developing that is being torn apart and that is literal. The logic that if a person doesn't support abortion, they should not have one is equal to saying if a person opposes murder, they should not commit it. We would not demand murder be legalized to preserve that "choice."

Pro-Choice is so protective of their concept of female empowerment through sexuality that they refuse to even allow bills to pass to provide anesthesia to a baby being dissolved, sucked out, crushed or ripped into pieces because it might strengthen the "its a baby" argument for the other side. We have to fight just to prevent a baby from suffering during an abortion to combat this stubborn mindset.

Pro-Choice advocates are often focused exclusively on the experience of the woman involved and refuse to even acknowledge that another person is being affected. This is the last stage in our leap from brutal savage humanity to enlightened beings who value each other equally and naturally. Abortion is the last piece of selfishness and elitism. It moves us from the mindset that we can determine who is valuable to society and thus worthy of life and freedom and who is not. When we can look at the smallest part of our physical history and recognize the inherent beauty in the creation of life, we will finally reach our potential.

In their own words from The Pro-Choice Action Network in an article titled *Personhood: Is a Fetus a Human Being?:* "Regardless of whether a fetus is a human being or has rights, women will have abortions anyway, even if it means breaking the law or risking their lives. Even women who believe that abortion is murder have chosen to get abortions and will continue to do so.

That's why we should leave the decision up to women's moral conscience, and make sure that they are provided with safe, legal, accessible abortions. Because ultimately, the status of a fetus is a matter of subjective opinion, and the only opinion that counts is that of the pregnant woman."[22]

Replace 'abortion' with 'rape' and 'women' with 'men' and then reread that sentence. How about "child porn", molestation or good, old-fashioned murder" *Regardless of whether a woman is a human being or has rights, men will rape them anyways, even if it means breaking the law or risking their lives.*

Even men who believe rape is wrong have chosen to rape and will continue to do so. That's why we should leave the decision up to the man's moral conscience, and make sure that they are provided with safe, legal and accessible rape options. Because ultimately, the status of a woman is a matter of subjective opinion, and the only opinion that counts is that of the rapist.

The justification of something genuinely wrong never removes the truth of why or how it is wrong.

Gay Rights: An Unnecessary Battle

April 7th, 2014 | Originally Published on American Thinker

As a gay American I am repeatedly warned throughout the media that my status as a citizen and my constitutionally held rights are at the very mercy of an angry, bigoted and unreasonable mob of Christian authoritarians controlling the country.

This is evidenced by the opposition to same – sex marriage and states like Arizona and Mississippi (among others) passing "anti – gay" segregation laws. Liberal articles declare that even my ability to receive HIV treatment is at risk, as did the *Huffington Post* in an article stating: "...restaurants could turn away same-sex couples celebrating an anniversary, and pharmacists could refuse HIV...drugs."[25]

Allow me to consider the weight of this claim and provide a reasonable prospective in response. The assumption is that if given the legal authority, Christians would readily exploit said laws to intentionally discriminate against gay, lesbian, transgendered or any other category of person they do not support religiously.

The result would be a world similar to pre – 1960's America in which black people were denied access to restaurants and other businesses. Naturally this would be a nightmare for Jews, women and other minorities who rely on the continued fight against conservative demands for domination of the public voice and public policy.

The curious thing, however, is that Christians currently have the ability to discriminate against gays, or whomever they wish, in all walks of life and yet do not take advantage of said power. America is a majority Christian country and so logically my personal experience, as well as the experience of all non – Christian Americans should be heavily restricted in terms of everyday access to goods and services according to liberal cries of outrage. Somehow, we walk freely and unmolested.

To examine the idea that, if allowed to have become law, the Arizona bill (SB 1062) would have allowed pharmacists to refuse HIV prescriptions, we must first consider the current state of pharmacists in America. Are Christian pharmacists currently or have they in the recent past refused gay customers or denied filling HIV prescriptions as a result of their religious beliefs?

Has a Christian owned pharmacist or store containing a pharmacy made a policy to selectively deny HIV medication requests? Have Christians working in the prescription industry boycotted, or refused to sell, produce or distribute HIV medications? Have Christian medical professionals or scientists refused to participate in the innovation of HIV drugs or actively stood in the way of their advancement?

Take a step back and see if any Christian doctors have refused to treat gay HIV patients or prescribe them HIV treatment. Are there Christian organizations devoted, even in part, to boycotting, suing, protesting or limiting the innovation, sales, distribution or fulfillment of HIV treatment drugs to gay patients? Do Christian churches, in any form, across the country advocate against HIV treatment for gays?

The answer is, of course, that all of the above would be ridiculous. Christians working in the medical profession simply do not have any concern whatsoever with assisting gay patients with HIV treatment, or any treatment for that matter. Christians do not have a moral opposition to treating gay people with any disease, let alone HIV.

These sets of questions can be applied to any industry across our nation. Are Christian restaurant owners currently refusing gays? Is there even a single instance of a Christian restaurant owner silencing and removing a gay couple from their establishment once it was discovered they were celebrating a romantic anniversary?

Gays are not denied entry into any public space owned by Christians. Gays are not limited to what they can and cannot purchase in any store or establishment open to the public. Gays are not excluded from Christian themed stores, restaurants or theme parks. Gays aren't even restricted from entering churches across the land!

To be sure, gays experience absolutely no limitation of their natural rights and this includes the right to bear arms, vote, or the right to free speech, assembly or religion. Gays are not restricted in legal protections, property ownership, reproduction, education, business creation, taxation, political activism or any other activity, civil or otherwise, enjoyed by all Americans. Actually, gays are not intentionally excluded under any law in the land.

Any law, policy or decision made by a business or government office that liberal gay activists cite as proof of their second-class citizenship can be more accurately understood in terms of discrimination towards single individuals in favor of married couples.

Classic examples of hospital visits, property transfers and adoption are misrepresented as "anti-gay" when they are actually issues related to being single. If a gym offers a "spousal discount" and a gay couple is denied, this is not an "anti – gay" policy. Any couple not married would be denied this discount.

The same can be argued in all other cases. Examples related to interracial discrimination are invalid. If a man and a woman of a certain age and status (not currently married, citizen) are eligible under state law to be legally recognized as married but a new law is introduced to specifically prevent a black and white coupling then it is understood as intentional discrimination.

Gay people are not intentionally excluded from marriage; the coupling was just not anticipated. Same – sex marriage is really a request to add to the current state eligibility requirements for recognition.

Gays have equal access to the same legal mechanisms and free market options all Americans have to influence desired changes in policy or law. Conservatives encourage and support this fully despite not always agreeing on the desired goal. Any addition to law or policy to benefit same – sex couples is currently possible.

To further the point, Christians do not oppose legal recognition or access for gays. The opposition to same – sex marriage has nothing to do with limiting access to property transfers or hospital visits for gays. If this were the case Christians would be protesting hospitals that offer services to gay couples, protesting legal firms that negotiate property transfers for gay couples after death and suing to nullify wills written by gay people designating property or funds to their partner or children.

Christians have no interest in interfering with the personal lives of gay Americans. Civil Unions are barely a concern at all and only become a point of interest when used as a tool to enforce gay mores onto public opinion.

The reality is that Christians, as a general group, are uninterested in discrimination and conservatives are typically focused on curtailing liberal overreach. Christians are not protesting gay weddings just as Christian bakers did not kick out gay clients preceding the controversy in Arizona. The issue is on liberal enforcement of their values as an absolute that we, as Conservatives and Libertarians, fight.

We oppose business owners being coerced into participating or associating with events they deeply oppose religiously. I, as a gay Jewish person, have nothing to fear in regard to my rights from Christian interference. The work of Christians and Conservatives alike is to ensure the natural rights of all citizens are preserved. There simply is no evidence to the contrary.

Pro – Choice: Defending the Right Not to be Gay

April 10th, 2014 | Originally Published on American Thinker

I HAVE ARGUED PREVIOUSLY that there are no specifically anti-gay laws, only laws distinguishing between single individuals and married couples. There is one law that I missed. California law SB-1172 *Sexual orientation change efforts* actually does intentionally and specifically discriminates against people based solely on their sexual orientation. The law states: "This bill would prohibit a mental health provider, as defined, from engaging in sexual orientation change efforts, as defined, with a patient under 18 years of age.

The bill would provide that any sexual orientation change efforts attempted on a patient under 18 years of age by a mental health provider shall be considered unprofessional conduct and shall subject the provider to discipline by the provider's licensing entity."[27]

Essentially, any gay person under the age of 18 who wishes to seek religious counseling for their sexual feelings is now prohibited from doing so. Liberals have effectively denied access to healthcare to gay Americans. This law effectively puts a "No Gays Allowed" sign on therapist's doors across the state. Individuals with homosexual attractions are now a segregated population in the psychological community; their freedom limited to what is viewed as best for them.

Obviously, this is hyperbole, but it is exactly the language used by the Left whenever it is even perceived that a law or policy is presented that may reduce the impact of an issue they hold dear. We can see this clearly with the "War on Women" rhetoric around contraception compensation, limits to abortion and religious freedom laws passed around the country.   Liberals are highly sensitive to even the smallest pebble placed on the road they are paving through America.

The difference is, however, that the *Sexual Orientation Change Efforts* law actually discriminates, denies access and isolates a vulnerable population from engaging in not only their freedom of speech but their freedom of religion. This law does deny access to available healthcare options, not because it negatively affects anyone but because it offends the liberal belief in sexual orientation as an absolute when facing the direction of homosexual expression.

When a man or a woman chooses to end heterosexual relationship in favor of a homosexual one, liberal culture cheers. This is viewed as a profound and joyous victory for being true to oneself. Despite the impact, it can have on an already established family or marriage is irrelevant to the individual happiness that is assumed to be won by the decision.

A homosexual person doing the opposite, however, is viewed as mentally ill, in denial, or as subject to the result of forces outside their will. The bill states: "The task force [Task Force on Appropriate Therapeutic Responses to Sexual Orientation by the American Psychological Association] concluded that sexual orientation change efforts can pose critical health risks to lesbian, gay, and bisexual people..." which includes a long list of every known negative emotion a human can experience including suicidal thoughts.

This is based on the belief that homosexuality is simply a part of "who a person is" and that it cannot be changed. It is also based on the assumption that any attempt to alter homosexual feelings or expression must be the result of coercion. These two beliefs are quasi – religious in nature as they defy any argument against them as innately harmful.

The population this bill represses is a small portion of the mostly Christian community, although it is also expressed in Jewish and Muslim communities as well. There is no wide-spread attempt or program designed to actively seek out and eliminate homosexuality through therapy on the nation's youth, despite liberal fantasies to the contrary.

The population affected is so small it is surprising the gay community even knew they existed. The only reason they did is because they have become obsessed with eliminating any view or belief around homosexuality as a whole that threatens their worldview.

In a fascinating examination of homosexuality throughout history, David Benkof writes in an article titled, *Nobody is 'born that way,' gay historians say,* that even gay historians are unable to find evidence of a singular and persistent homosexual identity in any other time or place in our world before the 18th century.

The essential argument is that while homosexual expression and sexuality were present in nearly every culture, there was no defined homosexual community in any of them. Arguments are made that this is due to long standing cultural suppression, but even in Ancient Greece and Rome where sex between members of the same sex was culturally accepted and common, we do not witness an exclusive sense of sexual orientation.[28]

In our current worldview, our culture views sexual orientation as an absolute, but this is a new phenomenon. From many Jewish perspectives, this can be evidenced by the very prohibition in Leviticus 20: 13 which specifically mentions sex between two men. The Torah (first 5 books of the Christian Old Testament) was designed for all Jewish individuals, but specifically men in terms of sex morality. It is just assumed that all men are susceptible to homosexual acts and therefore prohibits it specifically. It also assumes that all Jewish men should seek out wives and produce families.

But all of this is irrelevant in terms of freedom. It is fascinating to explore the topic on many levels, and it is my personal opinion that regardless of the outcome of the discussion (innate at birth, cultural, mental illness, choice, etc) nothing negative occurs as a consequence.

We have freedom that allows us to live the life we choose in America and that includes lifestyles others may not approve of. This freedom also includes those who would choose religious imperatives over personal desires.

I am comfortable with how I experience my sexuality, but I am not threatened by those who are not. Choosing a religious path is significant and it is insulting to assume a teenager is incapable of making a dedication to a religious path which includes choosing how sex impacts their lives.

Attempting to coerce a person to "change their sexuality" or go "gay to straight" is futile. Allowing a person to access the guidance and support they need to choose how their sexual lives are experienced is both compassionate and ethically positive. If an assumed straight person can struggle with their sexuality, so can an assumed gay person.

Choosing to live a Christian life or an Orthodox Jewish life, for example, and getting married, having children and adhering strictly to Biblical principles and laws is a perfectly appropriate choice which should be supported.

Our society should not be dependent on the mercies of the liberal religious worldview. Freedom of thought, expression and religion will inevitably lead to choices some do not approve of, but that is part of the culture we embrace and fight for.

If the gay community is truly devoted to a society that is open and free, they must first allow that freedom within their own community. Challenging the assumed is what builds creative and effective intellectual wisdom. Abolishing any view that appears threatening to absolutist worldviews is true suppression, not freedom.

No Such Thing as "Marriage Equality"

April 10th, 2014

"Marriage Equality" has become a popular phrase primarily used to intimidate opposition. While proponents of same – sex marriage view this as an endearing term meant to inspire justice, the reality is that it is fairly meaningless outside of its popular emotional appeal.

The term assumes that the various options for relationship combinations are on a level field but are largely discriminated against in favor of only a single option. The message is often expressed as "People should be able to marry who they love!" and "my marriage doesn't impact your marriage so why would you care?"

From a very basic point of view, the law really only sees people in terms of Single, Family or Married. Outside of these categories a person is a legal stranger to another person. We have legal methods of connecting strangers through manual designation, but automatic designation is only available for family and marriage.

A person can will their property to anyone (or anything) they choose, but their property will only be automatically transferred under the above conditions. The argument is that because gay couples do not experience the automated transfer process they are being intentionally being discriminated against. They claim this to be an issue of equality.

The only way to remedy this would be to recognize any relationship available as equal under the law. Most gay marriage advocates do not support that line of reasoning and merely want their relationships to be included under the "equal" category. Let me approach this topic from another angle. Imagine a person develops a long term and emotionally significant closeness with an older couple and they form a parent/child – relationship. I experience this personally.

If the parents were to pass on, despite the significant relationship involved, the person who feels as though he was like their son has no automatic legal standing in terms of their estate. If the couple had children, their children would automatically inherit the estate and be able to make decisions. The quality of the relationships are entirely irrelevant under automatic law.

To argue that it is unfair that the person in this parent/child relationship would not be legally treated as their son would be illogical. How could the courts possibly quantify that designation? Couldn't anyone claim to be the child of a deceased person in order to inherit their property? The laws are there for a reasonable exercise of judgment – not to validate emotional authenticity.

Now in my personal case I have designated the older couple in various legal documents to have authority to make decisions on my behalf and to inherit my estate if I were to die. I have done the same for other significant people in my life. This is a logical way to approach the legal nature of my relationship with them.

The reason many people support same – sex marriage is because they are sympathetic to the emotional nature of the relationships involved. The authenticity of homosexual relationships is not in question, which further deflates the relevance of "marriage equality." The issue from a secular point of view is a mere issue of legal definitions that best suit the needs of those who fall outside of the automatic process.

It is unnecessary to redefine what a parent is in order to conform to my personal deviation from the normal understanding. Whether or not my relationship is identical in nature to birth parents or adoptive parents is irrelevant legally. This is not a judgment on my relationship either.

From a religious point of view, I try to frame it as such: Jewish conversion is a legal status transfer from a Gentile to a Jew. A person must be trained by a willing rabbi, stand before a rabbinical council and perform specific religious rites in order to be considered Jewish under Jewish law. This new status provides access to religious duties and experiences.

If a non – Jew wanted to be converted in order to obtain this status and access to the benefits, but did not wish to involve a rabbi, be Jewish, adhere to Jewish laws or practices or engage in the religious benefits it would seem fairly ridiculous. Now imagine this being described as "discrimination" because Jewish leaders would not recognize this new legal status and the individual claimed he deserved "Religious Conversion Equality!"

Marriage is a significant religious life – choice that carries specific and long – lasting obligations. Romantic feelings are not the most important part of the institution. Without a religious context, marriage makes no sense. Everything from the very nature of sex to personal responsibilities to each other and to G-d are vitally important and only relevant under Holy Matrimony.

In many ways love is irrelevant to the promises made before G-d and each other and the fulfillment of those promises. People not intending to fulfill religious requirements have as much logical reasoning to engage in religious rituals as do non – Jews engaging in conversion rituals without the intention to be Jewish.

This is the very foundation of opposition to same – sex marriage, or any alterations to the institution. Even though many people who become legally married do so without any religious context, drastically changing the definition to further separate marriage from faith is both offensive and completely unnecessary. If the goal to to obtain the various secular legal benefits, we have mechanisms to do just that. The only other reason for insisting that marriage itself be altered is to prove a point. Unfortunately, that is the actual meaning of "marriage equality."

It is not an issue of true equality as gay individuals are not denied the ability to obtain a marriage license under current state eligibility requirements unlike black people were previously when they attempted to marry a person who was white.

It is not an issue of natural equality because there is simply no precedent for the religious binding of two individuals of the same sex under highly restrictive lifestyle obligations only relevant under religious pretexts. It is also not an issue of access to legal designations which can be currently easily obtained. It is only about cultural domination of a single point of view using emotionalism to intimidate dissent.

What would I advise Christian conservatives on the issue? Do what the Jews do. Orthodox Jews focus on Jewish marriage with intense focus on purity to Jewish lifestyle necessities. They celebrate adherence to this within their community and they are entirely uninterested in how non – Jews perform their own marriages. Christians should do the same. Re – focus marriage as Christian marriage and celebrate the unique binding of lives together for a singular purpose.

Remove the dependence on state and federal regulations and return to church – sanctioned unions. There is likely no stopping the reformation of legal marriage under the guise of "equality" and it will become utterly unrecognizable. Why participate in an institution designed to mock everything Christianity stands for? Forget Marriage Equality and focus on Marriage *Quality*. Liberals can never define your relationship to G-d and they can never win the battle to snuff out faith as long as people of faith own it completely.

Conservatism: The Best Choice a Gay Person Can Make

April 11th, 2014 | Originally Published on American Thinker

ACCORDING TO AN ARTICLE by *CNN Money* titled, *Gay people earn more, owe less*, on a 2012 survey conducted in consensus with studies by the Census Bureau and Experian gays make more money than their straight counterparts, have less debt, higher education and more equity in their homes. Gays also have a slightly lower unemployment rate in comparison to the nation as a whole. According to liberal standards, by making an average of $61,500 vs the straight average income of $50,054, a straight person makes $0.81 per every dollar a gay person makes.[30]

Gallup, however, found that when interviewed, gays report having less income, less education and report being less satisfied with their standard of living and economic possibilities than their straight counterparts. The Gallup survey notes imply this is due to lack of "equality" in marriage, employment discrimination and other factors burdening gay Americans.[31]

CNN Money as well as a corresponding article by the liberal website Slate titled, *Are Gay People Smarter Than Straight People?* both state that the reason for the improved financial stability in gay households is due to discrimination against gays which causes them to be insecure about their financial futures and therefore work harder towards better education, better jobs, better money management and debt balancing. By logical reasoning, being denied a "social safety net" seems to dramatically improve financial security and independence.[30,32]

Ironically, gay Americans seem to agree with conservatives under this mindset considering this is precisely the position conservatives take on financial and social independence. Without government interference, individuals have the capability of growing their skill set based solely on their own will and motivation, build businesses and careers and manage their finances more strategically. This level of independence and personal responsibility make anti-discrimination laws and regulations irrelevant as the individual acts on their own to insure their property, wealth and career.

Without the obsession for micromanaging every emotion, thought, word and motivation for all aspects of life to banish any anti-gay view, gays in general would simply be able to design their lives around whatever inconvenient barriers they may face and would use their influence to improve whatever processes they find cumbersome. They could do all of this with very little opposition since conservatives are uninterested in preventing gay people from managing their legal and financial lives.

The underlying story here is that despite the clear advantages held by this population, when interviewed they still identify as victims of their society. Instead of seeing previous barriers as springboards for entering an era of prosperity where bigotry could not impact them, they choose to marinate in the concept of being an "oppressed minority."

A business owner, regardless of their beliefs on homosexuality, is unlikely to refuse to hire or actively fire a highly educated, trained and motivated employee who could vastly improve their profit margin based solely on their personal life. The owner, however, would be smart to avoid hiring a person who defines themselves solely on their sexuality and who is likely to cause more trouble than add value by accusing the owner of discrimination at every turn. The law does not allow the business owner to make that reasonable distinction and so good gay employees are lumped together with bad ones.

Income gap analysis is fairly irrelevant in practice as there are no honest ways to evaluate the relative worth of one skill set to any one business model comparison. It is true that there is a large gap between wealthy gays and poor gays, but the problem clearly is not workplace or social discrimination.

The existence of a large number of wealthy gays illustrates that with all the tools conservatives routinely encourage as necessary such as quality and strategic education, debt balance and personal responsibility it really does not matter what social category you may fall into. In contrast, obsessive identity – based regulation, Affirmative Action, endless lawsuits, focus on inequality and discrimination laws limit the other portion of gays from succeeding. A person's worth becomes dependent on how entitled they are to a diversity position in any given scenario.

With ever-rising demands for higher taxes on those above the middle-class line and calls for even higher taxes on the childless in particular, a factor stated to be assisting the current affluence of American gays, this particular population should be very wary of liberal progressivism controlling the country. As stated in an article titled, *Tax the Childless* on Slate.com, "Who should pay more? Nonparents who earn more than the median household income, just a shade above $51,000. By shifting the tax burden from parents to nonparents, we will help give America's children a better start in life, and we will help correct a simple injustice."[33] The only logical outcome of supporting liberal policies is a shrinking income gap with the wealthy gays moving closer to the poorer gays.

Is it really a strategic move to support politicians who verbally advocate for same – sex marriage when those same politicians will also advocate for higher penalties for participating in it? The 2012 Experian survey states: "...when looking at married or partnered gay men, we see that their household incomes are over $21,000 higher, on average, than that of the typical married or partnered heterosexual man."[34] The term "married" relied on verbal identification. It seems fairly clear that marriage is not a good financial move to make under liberal control.

Liberal progressives consider the current level of success, education and financial stability enjoyed by gays in this survey as negative in principle. Their views and policies are designed to "equalize" the population more evenly, disallowing individual high achievement. Gays have had the most freedom, influence and success through utilizing conservative principles than they ever had utilizing liberal progressive principles.

It seems obvious that it is in the best interest of the majority of gay people to support conservative policies at both a state and national level. Supporting an emotionalized social cause may be fulfilling but it won't pay the mortgage. What good does it do us to have a laundry list of "gay rights" when we will be barely scraping by with the rest of the population in a decade's time?

Liberalism has gay people protesting in the streets, angrily writing about their collective torment, fighting to deny the rights of those they think oppose them, wallowing in self – pity and following the same path all identity grievance groups have undertaken. Gays find more fulfillment in deposing the brilliant tech pioneer, Brendan Eich, for his perceived thought – crime of opposing same-sex marriage[35] than they do in their own financial futures. More of us are willing to sabotage the very establishment that allows us to succeed for an imaginary victory for "equality!" Is the goal to stamp out all "hate" across the land only to sing around trashcans in our collective poverty secure in the knowledge we are all equal?

Conservatism allows individuals to build the life they choose without limitation. Liberalism convinces the individual they are limited as long as they are not part of a collective. The best choice a gay person can make is to support leadership devoted to removing obstacles (regulations, laws, government) so all people can succeed by their own will rather than support leadership that builds levels for each approved group of people to achieve equally.

The *Slate* article referenced poses the question: "Are gay people smarter than straight people?" in relation to the better financial and educational choices described. I would pose a better question: *"Are gay conservatives smarter than gay liberals?"* The answer is clear.

The True Legacy of Matthew Shepard

April 20th, 2014 | Originally Published on American Thinker

It has been 15 years since Matthew Shepard was murdered. I was in high school, and I still remember the unnerving awareness that being gay was now linked directly with being a victim. Leaving for school I tensed up at every glance or smirk I saw on my fellow classmate's faces. When I wanted to take a boy to the prom that year my dad demanded: *"Do you want to be the next Matthew Shepard!?"*

But all of it was a lie. The story was a lie. My fear was based on a lie. Yet the Matthew Shepard Foundation reports revenue upwards of $900,000 in 2013.[37] The Facebook page for the NO H8 Campaign posted a remembrance photo stating that the Matthew Shepard Foundation's mission is to *"replace hate with understanding, compassion and acceptance."* The foundation simply dismisses the evidence provided by gay journalist Stephen Jimenez in his book: *The Book of Matt: Hidden Truths About the Murder of Matthew Shepard* as offensive and apparently has merely continued on as if the revelation of truth never existed.

We now know that Matthew Shepard died in a drug deal with his gay lover that cold October night in Wyoming. We know the drug was crystal meth and we all know the terrible consequences of using that drug. His death was cruel and unjustified, but it was not a hate crime, and it certainly was not a brilliant light shining down upon the ugly realities of a hostile and violent heterosexual population threatening gay people. Yet why do gays still hold so tightly to this narrative?

The liberal mindset seems to be perfectly comfortable with emotionally gratifying lies as long as they serve a purpose. The incident emboldened the gay left to push for aggressive hate crime laws and despite being one of a small handful of gay bashing violence in the entire decade, the story has been continuously used as justification for gay fear of violence towards them.

Even if the story were true – word for word – it still illustrates a small and largely absurd scenario for any gay man to find himself in. Unless you were planning to come onto a couple of young, drunk and hostile straight men in a rural bar in the wee hours to engage in anonymous sex, you really didn't have anything to be worried about.

Yet, as was portrayed in the TV show *Queer as Folk,* a popular drama depicting gay people living in a heavily populated gay part of Philadelphia, gay bashings are considered common place! The show featured two story arcs surrounding violent attacks on innocent gay men by straight men. According to Gallup, there should be about 10 to 11 million gay people in the US. The FBI Hate Crimes report for 2011 shows 1,256 hate crimes against gay people in the U.S. That is about 0.01% of the gay population.[38]

A frantic report by Business Insider in 2012 titled: *There's a Disturbing Trend Involving Anti-Gay Hate Crime in the US* reports that most anti-gay crimes happen to gay men.[39] According to the 2010 CDC report titled: *The National Intimate Partner and Sexual Violence Survey,* Sexual Violence by a non-intimate gay man was reported by 40.2% of gay men. Any violence by an intimate same – sex partner was reported by 26% of gay men. Lesbians reported 43.8% in that same category. In fact, 28.6% of heterosexual men who reported being sexually assaulted were assaulted by other men.[40]

Where exactly is this vast threat of heterosexual violence against gay people coming from again? It seems more logical that the biggest threat a gay man faces comes from other gay men.

Liberal gay groups ignore this information and remain loyal to the narrative of anti-gay hate because it fits their overall bias against Christians and conservatives. The relatively low danger a gay person actually faces is inconsequential to the looming and never – ending story of gay oppression. The Matthew Shepard case more accurately demonstrates the statistical information for gay-on-gay violence.

Even the original story implied that the young men convicted to two life terms in prison each were secretly sexually interested and then reacted in "gay panic" resulting in the murder. Over time it turned into a story of angry straight men targeting an innocent gay man and viciously torturing him until he died as a way to promote the anti-bullying campaign. Liberals need an enemy, and they refuse to let go.

Personal stories rarely benefit an argument, but it is relevant to report that I was raped by another gay man who intentionally infected me with HIV. The entire history of violence I have personally ever experienced has come from other gay men in situations that allowed said violence to be easily accessible. My poor choices put me in danger, not some looming threat needing government – funded outreach programs. The intentional ignorance by the liberal gay community of the consequences of drugs and dangerous sexual appetites put gay people in danger, not heterosexual Christians quoting Bible verses in church.

The real tragedy of Matthew Shepard is that the true nature of his violent death has never been addressed. The consequences, however, have been perpetuated ever since by a culture too unwilling to admit its own failures. While desperately fighting an invisible army, the genuine monsters continue on in the background untouched by hate crime legislation or outreach programs on bullying. While straight people were being lectured on the appropriate ways to feel about and interact with gay people, gay violence, drug abuse and sexual abuse were pushed under the rug and away from the press limelight.

HIV infections among gay men account for 78% of the total and 63% of new infections in the U.S.[41] Liberal policies continue to ignore or dismiss this and other unpleasant information as irrelevant or they blame Christians and conservatives for causing the issues themselves through their "anti – gay" views. This is also reflected in the way liberal gays approach all areas of social and financial life. President Obama requested $23.2 billion in Domestic HIV/AIDS activities for 2014. Yet without looking to the source of the problem, no amount of money will help. Liberal policies continue to fail.

The real motivation, however, can be understood by a quote from Aaron Hicklin writing in *The Advocate* on the Matthew Shepard book, "There are valuable reasons for telling certain stories in a certain way at pivotal times, but that doesn't mean we have to hold on to them once they've outlived their usefulness."[42]

Liberals don't care about the consequences of their actions as long as it moves their narrative forward. In the best of motivations, they believe if the outcome fits their view of "justice" then the truth is irrelevant. Unfortunately for most gay people in America, the only people who offer them true justice and freedom are the ones they insist on hating in favor of a fairytale.

Orange is the Same Old Black

April 20th, 2014

I JUST FINISHED SEASON one of *Orange is the New Black* and I can honestly say it was just as everyone hyped it up to be. The stories are funny, depressing, thought-provoking and often emotional. One big flaw for me though was a predictable one. Of course, there is an "Evangelical" white trash Christian girl shouting aggressively about Jesus all the damn time. Of course.

Some of the things that impressed me were the unapologetic displays of in-group/out-group clustering, racism from non-white individuals and a transparent view of the flaws of our legal system. When the Hispanic group of women are mocking black people in shockingly racist ways, no one flinches. There is considerably less random physical brawling than you are used to on women's prison shows and in many ways the stories feel natural. I wonder how many women have gone to prison expecting this sort of environment due to the show?

Just as an observation, in my experience watching TV shows and movies about prison there is a fairly consistent theme. Men's prisons are full of truly dastardly and evil thugs who rarely have any saving grace to their character, and they wander in the background menacingly. The stories usually revolve around the personal revelations of a few who wish to change their ways while surviving the brutality of the others. Women's prisons are full of misunderstood women caught in situations they couldn't control and are now helplessly tossed away and forgotten.

Their stories involve a crime, but the crime is almost always sympathetic. They rarely focus on redemption and their stories are usually more focused on surviving the horror imposed on them until they can be saved or finally stand up for themselves and fight their way out through the legal system.

Men's prisons usually have friendly guards and women's prisons always have abusive misogynistic and sexually aggressive guards. This show is no different. The back-stories we have seen so far are all sympathetic and you can't help but feel sorry for them individually. Well, all except one. Pennsatucky is introduced as an aggressive, intellectually challenged Christian who provokes others in childish yet frightening ways. She is possibly the most awkward character in the show and her performance is almost satire. As far as I can tell the actress watched interviews of the women from the Westboro Baptist Church and then built her character.

Full Disclosure: I personally know very enthusiastic Christians. I grew up as one. It is not uncommon to see them openly praising Jesus. But nobody walks around like Pennsatucky. The character is openly ignorant, speaks poorly, is mindlessly aggressive and actually uses her faith as a weapon. She has a small band of like-minded followers who are just as pathetic as she is. In the last half of the season, she spends her time faith-healing while the other inmates mock her by pretending it works on them which leads her to believe she is "chosen."

Just to make sure the idea really sinks in, she is also racist declaring there should be a "whites only" bathroom while campaigning in an ironically racially divided representative government event (black prisoners elect a black representative, Hispanics have one, whites have one and then there is an "other"), she supports guns and refers to President Obama as "Hussein Obama." When the main character, Chapman, refuses to let Pennsatucky baptize her, she goes on a vengeful rampage devoted to killing her.

The show is smart, however, so it does sneak in some interesting tid-bits that manage to frame this ridiculous character into some kind of reference. Her back-story shows her as a white-trash meth-head in bed with her boyfriend and talking about getting an abortion. Her "why I'm in prison" glimpse is that after leaving the abortion clinic a nurse or somebody walks her out and comments that she should have a punch-card, five abortions, get the sixth one free. This angers her as she feels "disrespected" and returns with a large gun and shoots the place up. All the while a large group of Pro-Life protesters are seen near the building and they, naturally, don't flinch.

That provides us a view into the girls' personality. She is truly a sociopath and lacks the developmental ability to appropriately handle stress. She is loyal to no one, and she rarely thinks beyond her immediate emotional need. But, being an obviously liberal TV show, it just couldn't help itself and we find Pennsatucky being walked into a court room by a Christian legal firm to the cheers of the Pro-Life protesters filling the courtroom.

These are referred to as her "friends" by the Christian lawyer and we see her smile broadly as they stand behind her shouting and cheering her on. This is meant to show us that her obsessive devotion to Christianity is likely due to her association of it being the only thing that supported her, and it gives her something to fight for and to have meaning in her life.

If this took place in 1994 it might have been a bit more realistic, but even then, no group of Pro-Life protesters would be cheering her as a Christian firm represented her as some kind of hero for the cause. According to the Wikipedia page listing all known anti-abortion violence in the United States, "the U.S., violence directed towards abortion providers has killed at least eight people, including four doctors, two clinic employees, a security guard, and a ."[43]

Ironically, Pennsatucky's attack is more representative of the attacks on abortion clinics in the 1990's. They were committed by individuals or partners without the backing of any organization. She wasn't against abortion; she shot the woman for insulting her. The story is meant to make us believe Pro-Life supporters *believed* she did it to protest abortion and therefore raised her up as a hero. In reality no church, Christian organization or Pro-Life organization supported or praised these violent actions and always spoke out against them.

In the world of liberal mythology, abortion clinics were attacked by organized Christian terrorist groups. People in arguments today still refer to these attacks as proof that Christian Extremists or terrorists are equal in number and frequency to Islamic ones.

Mythology is built through repetition and so thank you, *Orange is the New Black*, for inserting yet another exaggerated and largely inaccurate portrayal of a myth, further solidifying it in the social mindset as reality. There is only one moment of real truth for this character and that is when she has a momentary lucid and rational conversation with Chapman where she vulnerably states that she wasn't just being mocked for her faith, but it was truly cruel because they made her believe in her faith and then took it away.

Interestingly the other Christians in the show are viewed naturally. We have the Gospel singing black girls, a nun and the Catholic Hispanics who routinely also burst into random religiously motivated behaviors but it is viewed as part of their cultural experience. Hell, even the transgender character is openly Christian, and no one blinks. Are there angry, aggressive Christians like Pennsatucky? Probably. The character frame isn't all that problematic outside of it lacking any counterbalance. This is especially relevant since the character frame is assumed to be a sufficient cover for large swaths of people.

Pennsatucky represents rural white Christianity. No other white character is shown as being different. The other white-trashy ones are just like Pennsatucky. A good example is the imagery of lesbian characteristics. We have several types of women who are either lesbian or bisexual expressed in the show. It allows the viewer to see beyond the sexuality. We don't just see any one of them as "the lesbian." There is no "black one" or "crazy one." We get to see a range of women with characteristics that make them unique rather than a selection of stereotypes.

The only real representation of a Christian is the nun who is quietly open to everyone and guides them as they allow her. Most Christians are like this. We like to peek into the Christian world and take away entire motives and concepts, but the reality is that a Christian on stage in a fiery monologue about the evils of sin is not going to be grabbing people on the street and doing the same thing. People who do that are crazy. Actually crazy. Mentally ill people who cannot distinguish between what is real and what is not grasp onto religious experience and use it as a format to express their paranoia. Real, everyday Christians simply do not behave like this.

People corner Christians into discussions, get the answer they provoke out of them and then use it as evidence. Its Confirmation Bias at its finest. The difference between this and, say, radical Islam is that the social structure in Islamic societies do not distinguish between religious life and everyday life and the radicals are not simply crazy people by themselves.

The threat doesn't come from the religion or the individual, but the groupthink that drives it to action. The religious experience is not the issue, the social group is. When you hear a report of Muslims committing a terrorist action after Friday services or see Muslim leaders cheering on the violence you are seeing a cultural collective. This does not happen with Christians, despite the mythology that they are the same in action and character.

Pennsatucky validates the fear many have as to the potential of Christianity. Without a counterbalance to demonstrate that this is an individual rather than a representation we simply continue on a hurtful stereotype. Unfortunately, the positives of the show become overshadowed by the biased portrayal and whole groups of people find themselves attacked and mocked in a show that is designed to exemplify diverse harmony and understanding of people as they are today.

It is possible to show white racism, the effects of rural poverty and drug use or strong religious faith without turning it into a joke or a villain. Even if the point is to create a villain, it's possible to do so without merely copying and pasting the same concepts over and over again. The problem is likely that the people who write the show think Pennsatucky is Middle-America Christianity. That prejudice is a hard one to break.

Redefining Marriage

April 22nd, 2014

As we know, the idea of marriage has become focused on equality and social meaning. As a culture, we debate, argue and bully each other over what is morally just for this institution. People who stand quietly, yet confidently, to preserve a traditional definition and expression of marriage find themselves mocked, accused of hate and shunned. To believe in the simple idea of a union between one man and one woman has become a civil rights battle all its own as even the professional lives of individuals have be threatened for holding such a belief.

For many the question becomes louder every day: *Should we continue to fight*? It is worth struggling so hard when our voice can be overturned by the whim of a judge or the angry mob reaction of a hostile media? With a looming divorce rate, frivolous celebrity marriages and the general idea that a wedding is merely a huge, exciting party, how can individuals fight for a holy union under the same name? It seems that perhaps it's time to rethink the entire argument.

I am a Jew. When asking my Chassidic rabbi about same-sex marriage he answered me simply: *"Why should we care what non-Jews do with their weddings?"* The simple, yet profound understanding forced me to look at marriage in an entirely different way. I am also gay, and I have long dreamed of my perfect wedding day with the man I love. What can I tell my Christian conservative friends then since my faith is neutral on the subject and my social identity is emotionally driven towards it?

Jewish teachings essentially exist solely for Jewish people. The reason being is that in Judaism G-d provided a higher level of responsibility to Jews that he did not provide to everyone else. Jews have 613 laws to abide by and non-Jews have seven. Marriage for Jews is entering into a sacred lifestyle promise to G-d that goes far beyond even love or emotional commitment.

We are to get married, have children and perform the mitzvot (commandments). The reason this is relevant is because from the perspective of an Orthodox Jew, marriage only matters to G-d when it comes to Jews. While non-Jews are supposed to be sexually moral, marriage laws are not really of concern.

Does this mean Jews discriminate against or don't care about the wellbeing of non-Jews? On the surface, Orthodox Jews refusing to marry an inter-faith couple may seem unfair, for example, but the reason is simply because entering into Jewish marriage holds a great deal of responsibility. Being in love is not enough to uphold a Jewish household. A rabbi does not want to bind two people together under a contract they cannot fulfill.

As explained by Rabbi Aron Moss of Chabad.org: "The chupah (Jewish wedding canopy) elevates the commitment beyond human limitations. The blessings made under the chupah invoke G-d's name upon the couple, and bring G-d into the union as a partner. You are married not just because you chose to be, but because G-d has said so. Without a chupah, you can have love, commitment and family—but it isn't holy. Only by standing under a chupah and marrying according to tradition does your union become sacred. Only after the wedding is your love blessed with the divine imprint of eternity."[44]

How does this translate to Christians who want to live a holy life by Biblical teachings? It means that, like the Jewish understanding of marriage, a Christian couple is not bound by social standards or acceptance. A rabbi would not marry two men not because he has any ill will towards them or their relationship but because he knows they can never be a partner in G-d's creation via holy marriage. Christians who believe that marriage is a sacred union can understand this as a unique part of their faith community rather than a representation of society as a whole. Where society fails G-d in Biblical teachings, it fails in marriage as well.

If a Jewish couple were to hold a secular wedding and obtain the proper licenses an Orthodox rabbi would not consider their union valid or holy. It truly has nothing to do with state recognition, benefits or "equality." Marriage exists for the sole purpose, for both Christians and Jews, of establishing a specific lifestyle designed by G-d.

Entering into this promise brings a couple into partnership with G-d to continue on creation and be a light unto the world. With each union comes new hope for the salvation of all people. Through the dedication to Torah, Jewish couples do not merely express their own love for each other, but they truly inspire and illustrate the love G-d has for humanity.

In some ways, it feels impossible to influence our society head-on and the negative consequences can be incredibly defeating. Perhaps if faith communities redefined marriage as a holy union unique to their religious standards and only truly valuable under those standards, the faithful who participate in them would feel far more pride and enjoyment. While it may not be possible to influence how the state defines marriage, like Orthodox Jews, Christians can bypass that entirely. By demonstrating how marriage has purpose and depth beyond just recognition of love, Christians can also show the world how devotion to G-d builds beautiful, strong families and communities.

In answering my own question on the topic, I realized that because of my faithful devotion to Judaism I would not attempt to try and force it to fit my own choices. Marriage, specifically, under Jewish law is something I cannot do with a male partner. That isn't a negative thing. We all can join G-d in his creation on his terms without ever being abandoned or shunned. The Christian community has a great opportunity to redefine what marriage can be by their own example through G-d's law even if it isn't represented by man's law.

Michael Sam: A Fictional Victory?

May 11th, 2014 | Originally Published on American Thinker

DESPITE WHAT THE NARRATIVE tells us, gays have an advantage in almost every social and financial area of American life. The NFL draft of openly gay football player Michael Sam further demonstrates this point. This week President Obama spoke of Sam stating: "From the playing field to the corporate boardroom, LGBT Americans prove every day that you should be judged by what you do and not who you are,"[46] The First Lady tweeted that Sam was an "inspiration to us all."[47] The NFL stated via the *SportsCenter* twitter feed that they admired his honesty and courage.[48]

Michael Sam was never discriminated against in football. He was not a star player forced to sit on the sidelines because of anti – gay demands. He never tried and then failed to play for a team based solely on his sexuality. He simply is gay and is a football player. Jackie Robinson broke through the baseball racial barrier when actual limitations were put on black players forcing them to join segregated teams. Jackie's achievement proved that his athletic skill was far more important than his race and was actually courageous.

There is no gay segregated football league that gay players are forced to choose if they wish to play football. Had Sam announced his sexuality only to be denied entry and then later, through demonstrating great athletic skill, been given entry, perhaps we could celebrate it as historical and brave. The fact that we only care about his sexuality demonstrates that his merits, as President Obama implied, are not in any way involved.

This is more indicative of the Left's infuriating fascination with the reality that gay people can do things everyone else is capable of doing. If he turns out to not be a great football player, will that be equal proof that gays cannot play football? It is utterly absurd that his sexuality is even involved.

The larger issue represented here is that gays have a privilege straight people lack. Being gay is enough to qualify a person as 'courageous' and an 'inspiration' for merely doing what straight people do every day. Being gay is not a disability. A gay person does not have to push harder, be stronger or think faster than his straight counterparts in order to be equal to them in skill. Liberals assert that due to homophobic bigotry, gays are excluded or discriminated against and therefore are not allowed to achieve higher. Why do we believe gay people are dependent on the opinions of others in order to achieve?

Today we have average everyday individuals who are only celebrated for honestly achieving great things and average everyday people with popular subtitles who are celebrated for every successful step they take without tripping. In our collective desire to prove to each other that we are open and accepting of gay people, we create a separate class both with advantages and the inability to function without constant praise and approval.

Liberals tell us that White Privilege is defined in part as: "...cultural affirmations of one's own worth; presumed greater social status; and freedom to move, buy, work, play, and speak freely."[49] This beautifully describes the gay individual in our society today. The actions, statements, opinions and personal offense of a gay person hold greater weight than that of a straight person. Gay Privilege is real.

Consider the reality that the most vile and inhumane thing an individual can do to a gay person is *think* they are sinful. Gays hold such a high status in our culture that we dare not speak ill of them for fear of devastating consequences. Ironic that a group held so high in society and incapable of being criticized could devote so much time and energy into complaining about "oppression."

Should a person be denied based solely on their sexuality? No. Should they be given access and praised under that same condition? No. The truest form of equality comes only when an openly gay football player is drafted, celebrated or criticized and analyzed without his sexuality ever being brought up. Michael Sam or his fans will never know if his success is based on his talent or merely his position as "the first openly gay" person drafted into the NFL.

In liberals' obsession with overtly demonstrating what should be inherent core values they minimize the uniqueness of the individual. A gay person becomes little more than a trophy whose purpose is to be exalted but dependent on those holding him up. A person has a privilege in being gay, but a gay person risks everything by being an individual.

For the majority of gays and lesbians going to work each day, spending time with family and friends and living utterly routine lives, normalcy is equality. While minority perspective can illuminate angles of an issue in interesting ways and our society still needs defined categories of personal experience, the only way gays will ever experience true equality is when we allow ourselves to be treated just like everybody else.

Rational Christianity:
The Benham Brothers

May 11th, 2014 | Originally Published on American Thinker

THE DAVID AND JASON Benham controversy has been well discussed in recent days. The left is always on the lookout for committed Christians expressing completely non-controversial points of views widely accepted throughout the religious and conservative world to be outraged over.

Their favorite subjects are those who represent the least actual threat based on said views and with whom the general public finds enjoyable. The media has been alive with shock and outrage over what the two brothers represent, both in terms of freedom of speech and the never – ending pursuit of "equality." The real story, however, is how the narrative of "extreme Christianity" is being portrayed.

The Left never seem to position their arguments as rebuttals to the Right; they merely assert their views are obviously correct and anything opposing is equally as obviously incorrect. An example of this is expressed by Rev. Susan Russell, a pastor at All Saints Church in Pasadena, California, "And this week HGTV made the decision that it does not want to give air time to two brothers who, when they are not flipping houses for profit, are proclaiming that equal protection LGBT families is "demonic" and protesting a woman's right to reproductive freedom."

The assumption being that clearly any criticism of homosexuality or merely being Pro – Life (or doing work for profit it seems) is inherently immoral. She finishes by declaring "As a Christian priest and pastor, my response is a big fat "Amen."[51]

Liberalism seems to have decided that the case is closed, and all opinion is settled on the general issue of what is acceptable and what is not when it comes to social issues. The Huffington Post discussing the Benham brothers put "*After Anti-Gay Views Unearthed*" in the headline of their breaking story implying the two had been caught doing something they preferred to hide.[52]

The brothers were labeled "Anti – Gay, Anti – Choice extremists" by the original website that caused the controversy, Right Wing Watch.[53] The brothers were accused of activism as though it had a sinister connotation. Their activism included participating in Pro – Life rallies, prayer rallies and other general interviews.

In 2012 David Benham stated: "We don't realize that, okay, if 87 percent of Americans are Christians and yet we have abortion on demand; we have no-fault divorce; we have pornography and perversion; we have a homosexuality and its agenda that is attacking the nation; we have adultery..."[54] at a pray rally at the Democratic National Convention in Charlotte, NC. This is what "extremist" Christianity looks like to the Left. But looking at the Bible, through Christian eyes, David is merely expressing the same concerns the writers of his faith shared.

1 Corinthians 6:9-11: "Don't fool yourselves. Those who indulge in sexual sin, or who worship idols, or commit adultery, or are male prostitutes, or practice homosexuality, or are thieves, or greedy people, or drunkards, or are abusive, or cheat people..." A very basic reading of Biblical scriptures will give the reader a clear perspective on both homosexuality and the value of the unborn.

Leviticus 20:13: "If a man also lie with mankind, as he lieth with a woman, both of them have committed an abomination...", Psalm 139:13 "You made all the delicate, inner parts of my body and knit me together in my mother's womb." And Jeremiah 1:5 "I knew you before I formed you in your mother's womb..."

As I understand Christianity, the purpose is to embrace the Bible fully and blend your life into the lifestyle prescribed within. It is absolutely a natural aspect of Christianity to be critical of the open acceptance of homosexual practices (the bible does not consider an individual to be exclusively 'gay') and even more so to be vocally opposed to the willful killing of an innocent person under the guise of "choice." These two views are in no way extreme when looking at both the Bible and Christian practice rationally. For a person to embrace this faith and then condemn those who hold to the very words of that faith is irrational.

There are no negative consequences to embracing this idea in Christianity as Christians do not act out against gay people or their rights. It is baffling to me how a person comfortable in their sexuality would find offense to the religious objection of a Christian to the physical practice of that sexuality. The Benham brothers are not accused of harming, attacking verbally or otherwise, discriminating against or even being dismissive or rude to gay people.

David Benham responded to the controversy by stating "We love all people. I love homosexuals. ...and my brother and I would never discriminate. Never have we — never would we," In the same article both brothers express: "Our faith is the fundamental calling in our lives, and the centerpiece of who we are. As Christians we are called to love our fellow man. Anyone who suggests that we hate homosexuals or people of other faiths is either misinformed or lying."[55]

The Benham brothers are not expressing *extreme* anything, they are merely practicing rational Christianity. They have shown no malice towards any group and have only exercised their influence towards important causes conservatives' support. Their only crime is that they verbally proclaimed what liberals find offensive. The brothers should be praised for their unique bravery and their compassionate and calmly positive approach to what can only be described as discrimination.

Jimmy LaSalvia, a well – known gay conservative, posted on his twitter account: "In 2014 opposition to homosexuality is far outside the mainstream. Just like racism and misogyny. All of those things will keep you off TV." He then further discussed this view in a blog post titled: *Consequences* where he lamented that "...the truth is that cultural standards and norms change over time, and they have found themselves way outside of the mainstream when it comes to the issue of homosexuality." He argues that viewers would be "...turned off by the anti-gay fringe activism of the Benham Brothers."[56]

It seems holding a basic understanding of Christian (and Jewish) sexual morality while also defending the innocent lives of unborn babies is now considered "far outside the mainstream." Perhaps this is a good thing. Why would anyone devote time to outrage over two brothers standing for their faith against great adversity when the liberal gay world offers far more relevant issues to oppose?

Is it so desperately important to preserve the *idea* of being gay as a social norm that we must attack Christians for pointing out the very serious issues we choose to ignore internally? Wouldn't rational, responsible and yes *normal* gay people side with Christians on these issues together?

The Benham brothers represent real Christianity and real devotion to faith. They deserve to be praised and imitated, not shoved into the corner to avoid the disapproving glare of the liberal masses. No reasonable person would need to distance themselves in order to prove tolerance. Furthermore, no gay person should see them as a threat. They are successful businessmen who help struggling people with their homes. They stand up for life and they advocate for a better safer world. They hate no one and they deserve our respect. They are what Christians are supposed to be.

Transphobia: A Reasonable Response?

May 19th, 2014 | Originally Published on American Thinker

"Transgender" has been in the social consciousness for a while now. Christine Jorgensen provided the first tangible image of a "sex change" in the 1950's and media has further explored the idea from *The Silence of the Lambs* (1991) to *Boys Don't Cry* (1999) to more recently *Orange is the New Black* (2013). As far back as our entertainment goes, opposite – dress has been a source of humor and surprise.

Transgendered characters often portrayed a sense of significant mental disorder or distress and an active dishonesty meant to be used as a twist at the end of a story. Discovering that the attractive girl is actually a boy is a staple in American humor.

The DSM -- 5 (Diagnostic and Statistical Manual of Mental Disorders) in 2013 changed the condition from *Gender Identity Disorder* to *Gender Dysphoria*. This was celebrated by the LGBT (the "T" is for Transgender) community as a victory for equality. Dana Beyer who assisted the Washington Psychiatric Society in making recommendations for the update states that the new condition implies a temporary mental state rather than a disorder.

This was important in order to remove the "stigma" associated with having a mental illness. As described by Beyer, "A right-winger can't go out and say all trans people are mentally ill..." The DSM – 5 also reports the need for this change as "Persons experiencing gender dysphoria need a diagnostic term that protects their access to care and won't be used against them in social, occupational, or legal areas...To get insurance coverage for the medical treatments, individuals need a diagnosis. The Sexual and Gender Identity Disorders Work Group was concerned that removing the condition as a psychiatric diagnosis—as some had suggested—would jeopardize access to care."[58]

If a person wishes to complete transition with surgery, according to most requirements including insurance coverage described in examples with Aetna and the University of California, San Francisco graduate insurance plan, that person must meet certain criteria.

These criteria can include multiple written approval letters from psychiatrists, a full year of living as the opposite gender, legal changes and hormone treatment. It seems that in order to obtain the physical transition to a new gender a person must obtain approval through APA (American Psychiatric Association) standards and the APA has manipulated psychological testing standards in order to justify surgical treatment.[59,60]

What is relevant to note is the movement itself seems trapped between its original motivation and modern demands for absolute self – classification and social acceptance of that classification. As described in the conundrum above, it is difficult to both demand sympathy for a disorder needing medical treatment while simultaneously demanding respect for the personal choice in identity a person makes at face value. As this guide to modern Transgendered thinking titled, *Seven questions about transgender issues you were afraid to ask* states: "Someone says she's a woman: fine. She's a woman. Period."

This same guide mentioned above argues that questioning a person's gender is itself offensive and the moral of the story is that people should accept whatever the individual presents exactly as they present it. Former *CNN* host Piers Morgan experienced the consequences of this offense after interviewing Janet Mock in early February of 2014.

The above guide describes this encounter by saying: "There were several problems with the language Morgan used. For starters, he repeatedly asserted that Mock had formerly been a boy. He also said that Mock had surgery to become a woman. Mock was a woman long before she had the surgery she felt she needed to reflect that. Part of the fight for transgender rights and justice is a fight for self-determination: to be able to proclaim who you are without anyone else adding caveats."[4]

There is a significant conflict of reasoning here that demonstrates how liberal thinking can be so irrational. A person born male who chooses to physically alter their body to resemble a female in order to satisfy their belief that they are female cannot later become reasonably offended when that history is merely pointed out as factual because it interferes with their preferred narrative.

As much as their goal is the acceptance of a person wholly as the gender they choose to be, we cannot demand that acceptance be absolute. Gay men and women struggle to openly accept Transgendered individuals who are also homosexual just as much as straight men and women do. Gender is not some amorphous concept without meaning.

As with the utterly unnecessary creation of "Cis-Gender" to indicate a person who is comfortable with their born gender, "Transphobia" is equally as unnecessary. While violence is never acceptable, a survey entitled *Injustice at Every Turn* by the National Transgender Discrimination Survey in 2011 reported staggering negative experiences from Transgendered individuals including a 41% suicide attempt rate.[61] With the fixation on absolute personal identification at any cost are we ignoring the impact this has on the individuals involved?

We live in a place and time where an individual can identify how they choose and obtain access to complete physical alteration to any level of their choosing. A person is absolutely free to transform themselves into whatever they like. But expecting the rest of us to feel shame over recognizing the distinction between their actions and normal reality is absurd. It is not wrong for a man to be uncomfortable dating a person who was born male but now physically resembles a female.

When looking at violence we see it as a result of discovery rather than targeting. There is a sense of intentional dishonesty and trickery when a man presents himself as a woman in order to obtain the physical or emotional affection of another man. Even with sympathy to the personal experience of a person who genuinely wishes to be the opposite gender, it is not a "phobia" to be uncomfortable with or disapprove of it.

Unfortunately, the Transgendered movement has taken the route all angry, irrational liberals take and actively bullies and shouts in outrage over the slightest offense they choose to experience. The Psychological authority is biased and motivated by political agenda rather than honest evaluation.

The significant emotional damage and social distress of Transgendered individuals is used as a weapon to demand further agenda – driven goals. This is not about protecting the individual dealing with gender identity; it is about redefining gender entirely to suit the current liberal preference. By recognizing the absurdity and rational difficulty with this demand we are labeled "Transphobic" and "Cissexist."

Regardless of the opinion if Transgenderism is a mental illness, a biological error, a personal choice or an emotional and psychological imperative we are free to embrace or dismiss the concept. By demanding that all people accept gender expression as relative to the presenter, we are stigmatizing natural impulses. It is wrong to demand that a person be labeled as a bigot for not viewing another person as that person demands to be viewed.

In the end liberals, do not create a more tolerant and open world, they merely create new and irrational categories of people to discriminate against. Appreciating the personal journey of an individual changing their gender is equally as tolerant as disapproving of the fluid manipulation of gender in the first place.

Standing for the Average Man

June 2nd, 2014 | Originally Published on American Thinker

AVERAGE MEN ARE THE most undervalued and maligned group of people in our society. As we have seen recently with the twitter *#YesAllWomen* frenzy, White Privilege and the frantic alarm of misogyny as a result of the Isla Vista killings, it appears average white men are the single most dangerous group of people in our country. *Salon* writes, "Every few years, the American public has to watch in horror as some white kid goes on a rampage..." and attributes this to "...the rage at the core of Rodger's horrific acts is not unlike the kind of middle-class, heterosexual, white male rage that drives much of social policy in this country."

The FBI reports that more than half (52%) of homicides are committed by non – white individuals.[63] Salon excuses this by stating, "...the problems of urban violence, which disproportionately involve young men of color, largely happen on residential terrain. Black men are not rolling onto college campuses and into movie theaters on a regular basis to shoot large numbers of people. Usually, the young men who do that are white, male, heterosexual and middle-class."[64] This, again, seems to diminish the active gang violence that routinely kills and injures multiple people at a time in places like Chicago. Unfavorable statistics showing 43% of Lesbians reporting sexual violence from their same – sex partners are ignored as well.[40]

The *#YesAllWomen* hashtag displays a feminist view of men as being obvious threats to women citing 1 in 6 women being assaulted each year. This statistic is used to demand that 1 in 6 men must therefore be rapists, despite statistical acknowledgement to the contrary.[65] Yet another statistic of 10% is used to demand: '*Not all Men? Imagine a bowl of M&M's. 10% are poison. Go ahead and grab a handful. Not all M&M's are poison!*'

Feminist tweets like "Every single woman you know has been sexually harassed" and "Imagine how exhausted I am dealing with sexism and misogyny. Every. Single. Day." displayed the remarkable insanity of it all.[66] A guide to "Rape Culture" details the many ways women face sexism from cruel, entitled men. For example, when holding a conversation with a woman: "If you pursue a conversation when she's tried to cut it off, you send a message. It is that your desire to speak trumps her right to be left alone."

It argues "Rape culture is telling girls and women to be careful about what you wear, how you wear it, how you carry yourself, where you walk, when you walk there, with whom you walk, whom you trust..." The overall theme is clear: "We refuse to accept that nice guys rape, and they do it often."[67]

From reading *Rape Myths and Facts* by West Virginia University, you'd imagine most men are exactly as feminists claim them to be. But like the concept of white privilege, when you scratch the emotional surface you see the many ways in which liberalism dilutes the issue. For example, Tolerance.org describes the perks of white privilege (and the disadvantages of not being white) as such: "When I cut my finger and go to my school or office's first aid kit, the flesh-colored band-aid generally matches my skin tone." and "When I stay in a hotel, the complimentary shampoo generally works with the texture of my hair." When I go to a hotel, I have to bring my own sunblock because my skin tone is so light I will easily burn at the pool. I am not even able to utilize tanning beds due to my hair color, skin color and eye color combination. So much for 'privilege.'

Under the same theme, a series of quotes from feminists on the difference between sexism and misogyny states: "To be specific, sexism is when men let you jump the queue and get on a crowded bus first..." only to toss in at the end "and then the poor dears, willy nilly, get crushed up against you as their hands "accidentally" cup your breasts in a frenzy of misogyny."[68]

At the same time feminists mock and dismiss arguments for arming women to protect themselves. Men who demand to have a say in the life of their unborn children are "...inadmissible; and where any man has tried to raise his voice he will have been denounced – as I have been – as an enemy of "a woman's inalienable right to choose." As discussed by Daily Caller Senior Contributor Matt Lewis: In defense of old white men "...I think we can all agree that it's wrong to generalize and stereotype people based on race and gender."[69] The problem is liberals disagree.

Underneath the layers of hysteria surrounding white privilege, misogyny, cis-sexism and any other concept liberals fabricate to justify their worldview is the reality that average, everyday people live lives completely untouched by them. Liberals care more about concepts than they do the real lives of the people they protect or malign. Murderer and rapist Clayton Lockett, as detailed by Ann Coulter, committed horrifying attacks on women and yet the liberal media wept for weeks over his prolonged execution.[70]

Elliot Rodger, who inspired the *#YesAllWomen* frenzy, is half-Asian and defined himself as "Eurasian" is the catalyst of proving "white privilege." Through rabid targeting of defenseless groups like white people, Christians or men they inoculate themselves from actual criticism.

The honest tragedy is that true victims get buried under piles of theory and opportunistic assault and the most vulnerable group in our society pays the price for it. Despite the mocking or the outrage from liberals over the idea that white men can be victims, the reality is that this group is singularly defenseless against all accusations against them. They are unable to reason against racism towards them because they are shut down with "check your privilege."

They cannot defend themselves against even the most absurd accusation of sexism or misogyny. At every turn, they are dismissed and demeaned with arrogant declarations that their arguments are invalid by default. White men experience actual discrimination based solely on their race and their gender.

Forgetting race, men in general simply do not deserve any of this. Regular men marry the women they love, raise children and work long hours to support their families. Single fathers make up 8% of our population without any acknowledgment.[71] Anti – gun advocates take away men's ability to protect their families. Progressive welfare systems and liberal feminism tax men's paychecks and require child support. Certainly middle – class and poor white men have no familiarity with any form of 'privilege' their skin color allegedly provides them.

Men who do not question their sexuality, are happy being male, are white, Christian and able – bodied are required to earn every single advantage they acquire. Without a victim status to fall back on, blame or use to their advantage, they must build their lives by their wit and skill alone. Being "normal" is in itself a disadvantage in our culture.

We should have a hashtag for *#YesAllNormal* to express the frustrations of being a healthy, responsible and balanced individual. While liberals spend their time fabricating new theories to solidify their own social privilege, average men work behind the scenes without any recognition. No one celebrates them for being a man and accomplishing anything. The final civil rights battle, in my opinion, will be winning equal recognition and appreciation for normal men just as they are.

Conservative Feminism

June 9th, 2014 | Originally Published on American Thinker

Miss USA 2014, Nia Sanchez (Nevada), just so happens to be a fourth – degree black belt in taekwondo and liberal feminists are not too happy about it. Cosmo editor Elisa Benson commented on this fact with this tweet: "I get that the college sexual assault problem can't be solved in 30 secs but still icky to pretend like self-defense is the answer."[73] The Huffington Post's very own Many Velez (editor) tweeted: "Let's hope Nevada uses her media tour to reiterate that teaching girls self-defense is NOT the best way to protect against assault."[74]

This is not a new conversation. In 2013 Zerlina Maxwell wrote: "I think that the entire conversation is wrong. I don't want anybody to be telling women anything. I don't want men to be telling me what to wear and how to act, not to drink. And I don't, honestly, want you to tell me that I needed a gun in order to prevent my rape. In my case, don't tell me if I'd only had a gun, I wouldn't have been raped. Don't put it on me to prevent the rape."[75]

Feminists seem obsessed with every possible detail around perceived male dominance when it comes to gentlemanly manners as told by Paloma Phelps, an intern for Feminists Organized to Resist, Create, and Empower: "It's problematic because the revival of chivalry seems to only consist of baseless acts of kindness that are meant to affirm a woman's place as less capable and [more] fragile,"

The article quoting her asserts that practices like "...holding open doors, lending a jacket to a friend who is cold or giving up a seat on the bus for someone who needs it more. It still implies that the practitioner is a noble "gentleman," and because men are practicing chivalry toward women, the concept places them in a superior position."[76] Yet, as described above, these same women find it utterly insulting to suggest a woman have the basic skill and confidence to defend herself against an attacker.

Feminism was conceived to empower women and create a sense of independence from men. Instead of relying on a husband for all of your needs, you could simply provide for yourself. Conservative women like Dana Loesch, Katie Pavlich, Michelle Malkin, Mia Love and many more effortlessly display this mindset in action daily. These women stand firm entirely on their own ideas and voices and illustrate true and natural female empowerment.

World shooting champion, hunter, Army veteran, mother, author and Smith & Wesson team captain Julie Golob discussing gun ownership for women states: "I find it hypocritical because we tell women that you know, you have control of your bodies, you have the right to say and do everything, you are equal but in this [gun ownership], you're not, you don't need that. It's so condescending and such an insulting concept. Instead we should be saying, 'Do what you want. Be responsible, be safe but if you want to do this or try this or be strong an independent, you can do that.'"[77]

Liberals are frantically shouting about "rape culture" and attempting to enforce a concept known as "the culture of consent." A California law, SB 967, calls for verbal or written consent to sex on college campuses as a way to "...change the equation so the system is not stacked against survivors by establishing an affirmative consent policy to make it clear that only 'yes' means 'yes.'"[78]

A feminist magazine called *FORCE: Upsetting Rape Culture* released a guide to consent, presumably to fulfill the now cliché demand by feminists to "teach boys not to rape." The magazine features "Consent Condoms" and proposed "ending survivor silence" by hosting a sexy underwear campaign which involved both boys and girls publicly displaying said underwear. As stated: "College students are the best people to teach other college students about how enthusiastic, consensual sex is the best sex."

It seems that the very same Zerlina Maxwell so offended that anyone would tell women "what to do" is enthusiastic about doing the exact same thing to men in an article titled: *5 Ways We Can Teach Men Not to Rape.* She advises, "There is no shortage of evidence that rape culture results from the objectification of women and the view that we exist simply for male pleasure. When a ESPN football commentator implies that the reward for being a star quarterback is that you get to have a pretty girlfriend, that takes away a woman's individual agency. She is simply an object to be possessed. An object there for male desire and nothing more."[79]

The #YesAllWomen twitter hashtag provides a live feed of modern feminist views and it essentially is all the same: Women are helpless against the will of men who are socially engineered to oppress, harass and rape them and women must rely on men to change their views and behavior so they can be safe. Under the guise of "empowerment" liberal feminists have taken every measure possible to effectively make women powerless in our society.

The idea that women should not be prepared to defend themselves against an attack because they shouldn't have to be in the situation in the first place is remarkably irresponsible. Predators exist despite a culture's best efforts and evil is simply a fact. The argument is emotional and, like the majority of liberal thinking, utterly absurd. When being mugged how effective it is to indignantly point out to the mugger that you refuse to defend yourself because he should not be mugging you in the first place?

The mind – numbing assertion that men, in general, somehow do not recognize that rape is wrong is a level of willful ignorance that merely perpetuates real sexism and fear towards men. If feminist's plan is to cross their arms and refuse to learn self-defense because they "shouldn't have to" there will always be more victims.

Ironically it is the very gentlemanly mores that feminists fight so hard against that is the true solution to the issue. Men in our culture were taught to respect women, to not see them as mere sexual objects and to treat them with special appreciation before feminists decided it was "sexism" and dismantled the entire system. But the most relevant perspective here comes largely from conservative women. Conservative women are not successful, safe and empowered in spite of men's continued "embrace of sexism", they are so because they choose to not allow it to affect their lives.

They do not define themselves by what men do or do not think. They protect themselves and view the world rationally which requires said protection. They have the ability to trust men naturally in their environment because they are self-assured enough to not be afraid of what the men *might* do or say. They are not victims hoping for some grand social shift that will allow them to both carry their own heavy bags and never face sexual assault again.

Conservatism teaches independence. At the very core, we are responsible for ourselves and women who understand that simply do not need feminism to define or protect them. Liberals have raised a generation of boys they cannot control and girls who are afraid to go outside. Conservatives have raised a generation of boys and girls who think for themselves, take rational precaution and simply do not spend a lifetime drowning in endless social theories that do little but perpetuate the same problems over and over.

We fight to keep people protected, enforce strict punishments for criminals and maintain our natural rights free from constant regulation. Fortunately, we have strong conservative women to remind us that despite the Left's best efforts, no one is a victim when they can take care of themselves.

Liberal Sex Ed and Rational Opposition

June 16th, 2014 | Originally Published on American Thinker

Sexual Education is often a go – to topic used by liberals to attack conservatives as being unreasonable and uneducated. The cliché of the sexually lacking ignorant Christian opposition is well known. It is equally accepted as truth that people, in general, were repressed and unhappy until liberal sexual liberation flooded the cultural mindset and freed them all. The argument over abstinence – only education implies that the only choice parents have is to accept whatever sexual education is presented or hope their kids don't have sex. The problem, however, is not in the nature of sexual education, but the agenda behind it.

In a piece mocking conservative opposition to sexual education beginning in kindergarten, Thinkprogress.org defended the program stating, "...students will receive age-appropriate information about wellness, anatomy, puberty, and sexual health that's tailored for every grade."[81] This is used to demonstrate that clearly conservatives are being irrational about the whole thing. Why would anyone oppose discussing wellness, puberty and sexual health that are "appropriate" for each grade?

What does modern psychology think appropriate is? *Psychology Today*, in an article titled *Is Your Child's Sexual Behavior Normal?* states, "...the vast majority of children, from a young age, derive enjoyment from genital manipulation...As long as children are nurtured through this time and taught to cherish their sexuality without flaunting or exposing it indiscriminately, it can be a healthy experience for the child."[82] Stopitnow.org, a website reporting to prevent sexual abuse of children, openly discusses children under age 5 enjoying sexual activity with peers.

The same *Psychology Today* magazine defines pedophilia as a combination of abnormal sex hormones to possibly experiencing sexual abuse as a child. It even implies witnessing sexuality may cause the potential pedophile to imitate. It opines, "The prognosis for pedophilia is difficult to determine. For pedophiles, these longstanding sexual fantasies about children can be very difficult to change."[83] At no point does the liberal mindset behind both concepts connect the dots to see how aggressively asserting children hold valid and equal-to-adult standards of sexuality and pedophilia could be associated.

Dan Savage, a well-known liberal sex advice columnist tweeted in response to Breeanne Walter's post: "@breeannewalters seeking out kinky sex in the absence of info about consent, reality vs. fantasy, etc. That can have disastrous consequences." and "Some young people are into BDSM. Shouldn't they have access to info about safe BDSM practices?"[84] Just as Richard Dawkins stated in 2013 that his own sexual contact with an adult when he was a child was not harmful, "I look back a few decades to my childhood and see things like caning, like mild pedophilia, and can't find it in me to condemn it by the same standards as I or anyone would today," he said.",[85,86] Savage tweeted in defense of Planned Parenthood stating: "...some kids are kinky. If you talked to kinksters you would hear from kids who were tying themselves up at 13..."

The driving issue is not whether adults should participate in BDSM or if it is right or wrong. It is ironic that the "rape culture" obsessed left would be so enthusiastic about sexual practices that are driven by the domination and intentional application of pain to the sexual partner often involving violent and humiliating actions. But, as in all consensual sexual activity, freedom does not restrict this with adults. The underlying problem is that the acceptance of this activity as being part of adult sexuality is not enough for liberal thinkers. Because liberals focus on "educating" adults on the possibilities of sexuality, they assume dominion over children in the same area. This is what conservatives oppose.

Sexual education is always described as teaching kids about their bodies, diseases, protection and healthy sexuality, but as we can see liberals define those terms differently than an average person might. The agenda liberalism promotes is the idea that sexuality is fluid, amoral and absolutely natural in all of its forms. Children experience sexuality early and should be taught to embrace it fully without question. Parents should encourage exploration and as long as everyone is fully knowledgeable and protected the experiences thereafter will be wonderful and healthy.

To deny children access to this is to set them up for dangerous experimentation, exploitation and emotional damage. The assumption is that because liberal thinking people view the world exclusively through sexuality, all people do and therefore everyone must be provided the fullest access to liberal sexual theory as an absolute.

The key piece that is missing, however, is personal responsibility. Where is the individual in all of this? Are we purely driven by various sexual impulses that can only be expressed through mindless action? Assuming every single theory on sexual development by liberal psychology is true, why are we bound to it? Liberalism seems to define itself by its lack of control over its environment. In order to survive one must be surrounded by warnings, labels, education, protections and emotional support. There is simply no concept that a person can choose differently.

Underlying the belief of child sexuality, pedophilia and teenagers engaging in BDSM is that they simply have no other option available to them and must simply do the best with what they have been programmed with. Sexual education has always been driven by the demand that "kids will have sex anyway!"

In 2011 the Heritage Foundation linked to an article about teen sexual behavior stating: "The toll that early sexual activity takes on youths' physical and emotional well-being and the association of abstinence with greater academic achievement all signal the importance of promoting the upward trend of abstinence through family, community, and public policy." It also concluded that "...numerous studies have documented the impact that parents can have on their children's sexual behavior.

Youths whose parents discuss the consequences of sexual activity and monitor them more closely are less likely to be sexually active, and teens who feel that their parents would strongly disapprove of their becoming sexually active are less likely to contract a sexually transmitted infection."[85]

It is important to recognize that if a young person respects themselves and is actively building their future they are less likely to take risks or allow themselves to be devalued. Abstinence is not about denying a person sexuality, it is about empowering a person to choose sexuality with purpose. We are free to explore sexuality as we choose, but why can't that include experiencing sex in a meaningful or spiritual way?

A young person has the opportunity to define their entire life based on how they view themselves in the present. Why do we assume sexuality is the only lens they have available to them? Conservatives do not oppose sexual education, they just simply do not want their children, or children in general, exposed to the liberal version of it. Young people deserve to be more than the sum of their sexual impulses.

Uganda: Selective Opposition to Global Anti – Gay Law

June 22nd, 2014 | Originally Published on American Thinker

THIS WEEK, THE UNITED States issued a message of disapproval towards Uganda's anti – gay law which can impose life sentences on homosexuals in the country. The White House described the law as an "affront" to "protecting human rights." National Security Council spokeswoman Caitlin Hayden stated: "The Department of State is taking measures to prevent entry into the United States by certain Ugandan officials involved in serious human rights abuses, including against LGBT individuals[.]"

US Senator Kirsten Gillibrand (D) spoke out against the nomination of Uganda's foreign minister to president of the UN General Assembly citing the country's treatment of gay people. She stated: "It would be 'disturbing to see the foreign minister of a country that passed an unjust, harsh and discriminatory law; preside over the UN body."[88] Several European nations have also cut aid to Uganda to show their opposition.

A senior administration official discussing the sanctions as stating: "The idea is to send a signal to perpetrators and would-be perpetrators that we are indeed monitoring, that we are indeed prepared to take measures, and that there are consequences[.] " Caitlin Hayden also confirmed: "As President Obama has stated, the Government of Uganda's enactment of the Anti-Homosexuality Act (AHA) runs counter to universal human rights and complicates our bilateral relationship [.]"[89]

Liberals use Uganda as proof of what a Christian majority voice can impose on an innocent population. The creation of this law has been connected to American Evangelical Christianity as the source. The Huffington Post, for example, implicates Rick Warren, author of *The Purpose Driven Life*, in this by stating he once visited with political leaders of Rwanda,

Uganda and Kenya and stated: "Homosexuality is not a natural way of life and thus not a human right."[90] This, they assert, proves he is partially responsible for inspiring Uganda to enact their anti – gay law. Rick Warren has spoken out against this implication and the law itself : "While we can never deny or water down what God's Word clearly teaches about sexuality, at the same time the church must stand to protect the dignity of all individuals – as Jesus did and commanded all of us to do."[91]

Uganda is categorized as a Christian country but is largely Catholic and Anglican; remnants of British Colonialism. The Anglican Church of England is the established church of England. It remains a mystery as to how England does not also have an equal anti – gay law punishing homosexuality with life in prison.

To the point, no other Christian majority country has a law even similar. Despite this, Reverend Dr. Kapya Kaoma, an Anglican Priest and citizen of Zambia insists: "...the influence of U.S. evangelical culture warriors has been felt across sub-Saharan Africa.

The Christian right has been involved in legislative or constitutional efforts to crack down on the LGBT populations of Kenya, Liberia, Namibia, Nigeria, Malawi, Rwanda, Zambia, and Zimbabwe as well. Uganda's Anti-Homosexuality Bill has become a kind of template for other countries, including Nigeria and Liberia, where similar laws have been proposed." As an interesting perspective, the same Reverend Kaoma observed that: "The nuclear family that Western conservatives promote is foreign to Africans."[90]

In contrast, President Obama in 2010 on the official White House website in relation to a visit with the King of Saudi Arabia: "I want to welcome His Majesty King Abdullah to the White House, and I'm very pleased to be able to return the extraordinary hospitality that he showed me and my delegation when we visited Saudi Arabia..." he gushed "On behalf of the American people, welcome. We appreciate your friendship. And we appreciate your good counsel and look forward to continuing to work together to strengthen the strong bonds between our two countries."

Saudi Arabia, to which even the Huffington Post laments, has an exceptionally strict punishment for those accused on homosexuality. A man who engages in homosexual acts can be stoned to death and the official religious police regularly arrest large groups of men gathered privately for "deviant" behaviors and routinely sentence them to jail time or flogging.

Muslim countries considered allies to the United States that have strict and open anti – gay laws include Qatar, United Arab Emirates, Afghanistan, Kenya, Pakistan and Yemen. Liberal favorites such as Syria, Gaza and Iran also strictly punish those accused and convicted of homosexuality.

While the gay left celebrates symbolic actions such as sanctions on Uganda and President Obama promising to sign an executive order prohibiting discrimination against LGBT workers at companies that are federal contractors, utterly unnecessary, the real issues of human rights across the globe are ignored.[92]

As with Russia, it seems the gay left is only concerned about anti – gay policy when it coincides with an agenda they already support. Both cases involved attitudes liberals love to associate with all Christians, Republicans and conservatives and therefore fits their established narrative of a dangerous world haunted by fundamentalist Christianity.

Just as their obsession with the Westboro Baptist Church as evidence of Christian extremism rampant throughout the country demonstrates how far from reality they manage to travel when expressing concern and outrage, the utterly flippant ignorance of Islamic persecution of women, Jews, Christians, Hindus, Buddhists, Apostates and yes, gays is remarkably offensive.

It goes without saying that Uganda's law is unjust and is an affront to human rights. All people deserve the ability to live freely. But the United States is either the colonial enforcer of Western values or it is not.

We cannot smugly demand that we have no right to criticize other culture's values and then selectively and simultaneously demand those same cultures adhere to our version of gay rights. Gays are not in peril because of a handful of Christian leaders preaching the evils of homosexuality from their pulpits. They are in danger because they live in a part of the world where the basic idea of human freedom is alien.

All people are in danger as long as governing bodies tightly constrict the lives of their citizens, especially with religious authority. In today's world, this is mostly expressed through Islamic governance.

Liberals want to hold signs, create hashtags and indignantly blather on about how things should be, but actively oppose, fight and dismantle any attempt to actually fix the problem. To make matters worse they utterly refuse to recognize the true enemy while frantically pinning strings to the wall in a desperate attempt to prove Christianity as the villain.

Homosexuality is illegal in 37 African countries. One of them has a Christian majority and no other Christian majority country on Earth mimics it. There are 49 Muslim countries and roughly 36 of them criminalize homosexuality. Why would the one country on Earth, devoted the most to enforcing LGBT rights focus exclusively on the only Christian country guilty of violating them? How is it a victory for gay rights and human rights everywhere if that focus is intentionally blind and arguably apologetic to the vastly larger number of countries who actively engage in what only Uganda is punished for?

Border Crisis: An Opportunity for Conservatism

July 10th, 2014

THIS WEEK GLENN BECK announced he would provide hot meals and toys to the children currently being held at centers across the southern border. His actions drew controversy, and many have shared concerns the act of kindness will only encourage more children to cross the border illegally. While the Obama administration seeks to obtain $3.7 billion in aid to the border centers and both Democrats and Republicans call for immediate action to stop the flow of illegal immigrants, there is a wide-open area of opportunity conservatives are missing.

Liberals have recently begun attacking anti-amnesty supporters by demanding compassion for the children who have made the remarkable and dangerous journey to our border. *The New York Times* states: "The killings are a major factor driving the recent wave of migration of Central American children to the United States, which has sent an unprecedented number of unaccompanied minors across the Texas border."

A quote in the article reads: "The first thing we can think of is to send our children to the United States," said a mother of two in La Pradera, who declined to give her name because she feared gang reprisals. "That's the idea, to leave."[93]

NBC News reports, "In the last five years, the number of kids coming through the doors who are victims of violence has tripled. On a busy night, Dr. David Mendoza might treat six or seven kids who have fallen victim to Honduras' crime epidemic. "We see younger kids affected by violence — 12, 13, 14 years old,"[94] The *Huffington Post* states, "The president acknowledged earlier this week that the situation had reached crisis levels on the border, as children from Honduras, Guatemala and El Salvador flee deepening poverty and violence."[95]

The U.N. High Commissioner for Refugees said it believes "the U.S. and Mexico should recognize that this is a refugee situation, which implies that they shouldn't be automatically sent to their home countries but rather receive international protection."[96]

The United Nations Office on Drugs and Crime reports "Latin America as a region has the highest rate of criminal violence in the world[.]"[97] Latin America and the Caribbean have 13 of the top 20 homicide rates in the world. The Human Rights Watch website reports on multiple areas of crime, abuse, child trafficking and other human rights horrors in South America.

While using this information to shame Republicans into accepting amnesty under extreme social pressure, Democrats and liberals do not seem to realize they are painting themselves into a tight corner. By so aggressively riling up sympathy for the horrific conditions these children have escaped from, they betray a vital aspect of their core values.

Liberals are unreasonably incapable of criticizing other culture's treatment of their own citizens under their *'you can't judge another culture'* or *'you can't impose your values onto others'* mantras. While currently using this emotional argument to condemn anti-amnesty foes, they in fact demonstrate their own incredible cruelty and negligence. If they are so concerned with these on – going abuses, why aren't they acting to stop them?

President Obama demanded sanctions for Uganda due to their strict anti – gay law, but not a single sanction has been applied to any South American country. In May of this year Secretary of State John Kerry, made a weak threat of sanctions against Venezuela over the crack – down on protestors by stating, "Our hope is that sanctions will not be necessary."

And "But Congress is discussing the sanctions, Kerry said, and it is up to Maduro [President of Venezuela] and others to "make the decisions that will make it unnecessary" for sanctions to be imposed."[98] While Obama lectured Israelis on building homes and towns in Judea and Samaria[99], he has not even mentioned the human trafficking, drug cartels or homicide rates of Latin America.

Truth be told, the nightmarish human rights violations of South America only seem relevant when useful as weapons of emotional war. This is, however, an advantage for conservatives. Conservatives alone speak out against the atrocities around the world the liberal media ignore. Conservatives relentlessly cry in outrage over the terrorism of Gaza, the human cruelty of China and North Korea and the anti – gay, anti – woman, anti – Christian and Jewish horrors of the Muslim controlled Middle East.

The problem is we are waiting for the left to support us and join our fight. It is time we reposition the illegal immigration issue as one of genuine human rights being violated below our border. The details and methods of immigration reform, amnesty and what to do with these children will be played out in politics, but there is an amazing opportunity for us to demonstrate the true values of conservatism in this time.

Democrats rely on the old prejudices and the tired lines of xenophobic and racist Americans who hate immigrants to float them through the next few elections. They truly believe they can milk this crisis and sacrifice these children to push them over their goal. Ann Coulter has brilliantly described in a column titled, *GOP CRAFTS PLAN TO WRECK THE COUNTRY, LOSE VOTERS*, how massive amnesty will wreck our country and she is right, but we can fight back.[100]

Conservatives have the chance to change the message, own the processing of these children and through charity and goodwill find homes, teach them and show them kindness. We can build in these children the hope of America we know lives deep in our collective spirit. The danger is allowing liberals to absorb them into the welfare system only to be used as pawns and a drain on society.

Conservatives can run on fighting the true injustices below our border, demanding boycotts, sanctions and cutting off trade to these abusive countries. We can demand that no child should be forced to flee thousands of miles to perceived safety.

We can stop unskilled and poor immigrants from becoming cheap labor by utilizing Free Market principles that will allow them to work and build their lives. The world can be just like America. The world can be free, but the Progressives and Socialists will not make that happen. Our leaders can use their influence and America's strength to rebuild our world and we can do that one child at a time.

I think of the children fleeing Nazi Germany and I can genuinely sympathize with what they must be experiencing. Abandoning everything they know to reach what they can only hope is freedom and safety. It is not fair. It is not even legal. But it is happening, and we have the opportunity to be different than the rest of the world. We can show kindness.

Liberal compassion is servitude and dependence on the state. Conservative compassion is giving help and safety and building strong lives through personal responsibility and charity. The battle has long been over the lawlessness of our President and the genuine danger of a poorly secured border.

The highest wall will not keep out the truly evil, but a strong and determined force can beat it back. Every person on Earth has the G-d given rights of freedom we cherish. That is what we were founded on. It is time America took action to make the world safe and free, not bow to the pressure or block everyone else out.

Daniel Pierce: Newest Gay Fake Victim

September 1st, 2014 | Originally Published on American Thinker

Daniel Ashley Pierce became a viral gay hero this week when a video he secretly recorded was picked up by the gay magazine *Advocate* titled *WATCH: 'Christian' Family's Terrifying Response to Son Coming Out.* The article opens with this ominous description: "A 19-year-old gay man is safe and staying with a family friend in Atlanta, Georgia, after suffering physical and verbal abuse at the hands of his stepmother, father, and grandparents when he told them he was gay."

The article goes on to say the video provides a "...chilling first-hand look at the violence and rejection that can result when parents don't accept their child's sexual orientation.»102

This narrative, naturally, plays directly into the popular myth of an oppressive and exclusive Christian intolerance for gay family members. As the fable goes, the heartless and cruel family gang up to give the gay child one last chance to repent before they disown him forever. As *Advocate* implies, this is common and the likely reason for so many gay homeless youths in the country.

This story is amplified due to the nature of the encounter which Pierce states was an intervention to attempt to convince him to undergo ex-gay therapy. As one commenter on the article put it *"This sounds like a typical coming out in a Christian fundamentalist family. And it is NOT shocking they all have Southern accents!"* liked 136 times.

The story was picked up by *BBC News* and Pierce was interviewed by *CNN*. The *CNN* transcript begins with: Grandmother: "You have made a choice." and the father saying "You're a disgrace." Pierce objects demanding he has been gay "...from the moment I come out of my mother's uterus. I have been that way." The *CNN* Dr. Drew interview quotes a man named Schacher involved in the discussion describing the video as such: "Oh, Dr. Drew, it made me skin crawl. It made me nauseous.

So, yes, at the end of the video it started to get heated and the teenager -- he remained poised and calm and continued to say it's not a choice. This is who I am. And then one person started to beat him and then another person you hear kind of cheering on the beating and he's saying, stop it, stop it,..."[103]

Pierce seems to have turned the video portion on at the beginning of the conversation and it is largely audio. His family is surrounding him, and his grandmother begins, not by condemning but by saying *"First I want to say that I love you."* She confirms she has known he was gay since he was a small boy, but nevertheless her faith states he has a choice in how he lives his life.

He responds by repeatedly and smugly dismissing her statements arguing he has taken a biology class and it has been confirmed by "scientific studies" that personality is developed within the first six weeks and there is nothing one can do to change that. The grandmother contends that G-d's word says otherwise to which he arrogantly replies: *"Well scientific studies trump G-d's word."*

The grandmother then firmly states that if he chooses to continue on as he is he is no longer welcome to live in her house. He states he will move out in a few days by midnight and asks his mother in an obviously sarcastic way if he can live in her basement. She apparently indicates no as he responds *"well that isn't very motherly."*

The conversation escalates quickly when his stepmother challenges him on previous conversations, he had on the topic with her to which he immediately begins shouting, cursing and physically moves towards her. He then engages in aggressive name calling and what is viewed in shaky physical confrontation in which several other family members attempt to break up the mutual attack.

There are several important components to point out. First, his age straddles 19 to 20, but 'teen' sounds better for the story. He did not 'come out' at this taping and the confrontation was not the result of the family's reaction to the news. He had been open with his family for almost a year and the original coming out went without incident. In fact, the BBC reports his family was 'supportive' and his stepmother responded 'positively.'[104]

He was in a long-term relationship which he proudly displayed on his own social media. In the Dr. Drew *CNN* transcript it is stated that Pierce's father was feeling shamed due to his son posting 'bad things' about him online but does not go into detail.

The Advocate, the *BBC* and *CNN* take the opportunity to divert the scenario's details towards supporting the discussion of LGBT suicides and runaways and spend most of their words detailing generalities of why it is wrong to be abusive towards gay teenagers. The problem, it seems, is that this story just doesn't fit that desired outcome. The narrative is that Pierce, like this assumed mass of other LGBT teenagers, was kicked out into the cold *just because* he was gay. Ironically the video evidence tells a different story.

When watching, it is easy to understand the family's discomfort and tension around this issue. While it is worth pointing out that a family intervention to try and dissuade a gay family member from being gay is an unusual and difficult scenario, it is equally important to recognize the inherent family support involved. Pierce is confrontational, arrogant and snotty throughout the encounter.

He makes no attempt at finding common ground or hearing his family's point of view. His view is that if the others do not fully agree with his version, they must be attacking him. The video indicates multiple conflicting and tense exchanges with various family members and his father's humiliation via his son's Facebook messages. Daniel Ashley Pierce appears to be looking for a fight with his family more often than not.

The underlying morality play here is that we are supposed to judge the family for not embracing Pierce exactly as he is. What is really being told, however, is the story of liberal arrogance in the face of disapproval. Why would a rational person instigate a conflict like this? Even if he were dealing with cold-hearted crazed fundamental religious zealots, why was it necessary for him to continue fighting to make them view the world through his perception alone? Couldn't he have quietly lived his life, respecting his grandmother's wishes in her house and worked towards building his life outside of it? We all decide how our families will fit into our lives. That is what grown-ups do.

Unfortunately, liberalism rewards those who pick a fight to prove a narrative. As of this writing, Pierce's Gofundme campaign has raised roughly $90,000 dollars. One person donating $100.00 states: "Daniel, you have shown the world strength and maturity in the face of what can only be described as ignorance. Your video brought tears to my eyes, as well as our global community's response to your experience. You are a role model for us all..." Rational disagreement, family ties, personal responsibility and mutual understanding, it seems, will not make you a hero in today's liberal viral world.

Christian Faith is Not Hate

September 7th, 2014 | Originally Published on American Thinker

LIBERALS HAVE FOUND A greater threat to the world than even ISIS: A Baptist pastor quoting the Bible. On September 3rd, 2014, dozens of liberal websites all posted some version of the same sentence: *"Megachurch Pastor calls for the death of gays!"* In a remarkable display of mass hysteria coupled with mind-blowing dishonesty, the articles all claim Pastor Robby Gallaty of Brainerd Baptist Church, aggressively and hatefully called for gays across America to be discriminated against and brutally killed.

The Daily Beast referring to Gallaty as the 'hateful pastor', "Don't be too shocked by megachurch minister Robby Gallaty's hateful sermon. There's a hard core of evangelicals that aren't evolving on homosexuality, let alone same-sex marriage."[106] *The Raw Story* posted an article titled *TN pastor vows not to 'repent' for homophobia: God says gays 'must be put to death'* which stated: "A pastor of a large Southern Baptist church near Chattanooga, Tennessee said this week that Christians would never repent for discriminating against gay people like they had for racism because African-Americans could not change the color of their skin."[107]

The most charming article, which actually contains the video in question, on *Addicting Info* said "And why should innocent gays and lesbians be put to death? Well, according to Gallaty, they have made the choice to be gay, thus rebelling against God's plan. Touching on the comparisons some Christians make in to racist beliefs and homophobic beliefs, Gallaty responded just as you'd think; insulting those who can see a legitimate comparison between two hatreds."

The *Addicting Info* article, spread around facebook due to its particularly aggressive and alarmist tone, contains the following gems: "I guess the commandment "Thou shalt not kill" doesn't ring true to Gallaty, who has proven himself to be another faux Christian who blankets his hateful beliefs in the word of God. But don't say that to the religious right.

They'll jump to his defense faster than anything else. Why? Because religious freedom, that's why.", "Just another mega church moocher who will peddle anything to keep banking off stupid people" and "As he preaches the genocide of gays, I wonder if he will touch on the fact that he sinning as he wears a pair of denim jeans and a cotton shirt. He probably won't though because that doesn't count in his tiny world of knowledge."[108]

Interesting note, Pastor Gallaty is not wearing jeans in the video. Watching the video provides a slightly different story than the one described above. Pastor Gallaty is shown reading a list of forbidden sexual activities in Leviticus which includes homosexual acts. He goes on to describe what the Bible says is the punishment for homosexual practices. He at no time advocates carrying out the death penalty for gay people. As is common with most Biblical study, including my own Torah study just this weekend, it is important to understand the significance of activities G-d designates with the death penalty.

From the articles, it would appear the video would then continue on an aggressive rant celebrating the joy Christians can have in executing gays for G-d. Unfortunately for liberals, Pastor Gallaty disappoints which brings us to their next hysterical proclamation: The pastor says gays deserve to be discriminated against because they can choose to be gay! What he says is that there is a separation between homosexual activity and the person engaged in it.

From the Biblical references, he states that G-d refers to homosexual *practices* rather than homosexual *people*. He devotes a strongly empathetic discussion to the deep desires and struggle people with same-sex attraction experience while balancing their faith. He compares it equally to not only his own personal desires and struggles, but to that of all humanity. His obvious point is that as a 'child of G-d', the person with homosexual impulses is not 'gay' as much as he is a person who can choose how to act on said impulses.

He attempts to make a clear separation between inborn physical qualities such as race and gender and controllable actions to demonstrate what the fallacy is in the homosexual identity. He never even implies gay people should be treated poorly or even differently. He is quoted in the video saying, *"It's the most lethal attack we have today against the family,"*, *"And if the enemy can ruin the family, he wins."*

He is quoting a rabbi and places it into the larger context that a homosexual identity attacks not only the family structure but also what G-d intended for mankind. While debatable, it is a recognizable consequence of fluid identity, sexuality and politically correct appeasement that the 'family' in any religious context is severely altered culturally.

But again, he makes clear this is not an issue of the individual, but of the social construct of a homosexual identity that causes said issue. At the end of the video he indicates that all Christians must take a higher road and must choose to follow G-d regardless of their personal struggles or desires.

There is absolutely nothing in the video presented that is threatening, hateful, cruel or the result of ignorance. A person may be offended and there are certainly points to be debated but that is not evidence of 'hate.' What is remarkable is the level of panic and aggression towards this man who is not only merely reading aloud the word of his faith but is compassionately discussing ways to overcome personal struggles to better adhere to it. The simple statement of that faith is enough to be categorized along with Islamic terrorists currently beheading innocents and burying children alive.

To be very clear, even if he were to call for the death of gays, it is inconsequential if no one acts upon it. For a reference of the ineffective danger to gays across America due to hateful speech, just see the Westboro Baptist Church. If a person believes their sexuality is a permanent and solid part of who they are or completely defines their personality, why would it possibly matter what a Pastor says about the Christian perspective on the topic? Is the mere existence of ideas found offensive such a threat the entire liberal and gay internet must attack it simultaneously?

Pastor Robby Gallaty is a strong and confident religious leader speaking to what he believes to be true, and he is doing so with compassion, honesty and sincerity. Nothing in this man's voice or action conveys malice. It is vital that men and women like him not be shamed into silence to satisfy the irrational insecurity and bigotry of the left willing to openly lie about a video they describe in the same article.

A Gay Jew Goes to Church

September 7th, 2014 | Originally Published on American Thinker

CHURCH, I AM TOLD, is a dangerous place to be. *"Two out of three Americans believe gay people commit suicide at least partly because of messages coming out of churches..."* CNN reported in 2010. Dan Savage, a gay activist, is quoted as saying he remembers "...being told to go home and commit suicide and that he was going to hell," confirming the study's findings stating it "totally jibes with my experience and that of millions of other gay and lesbian people."[110]

The New York Times reporting on the suicide of Tyler Clementi in 2012 described how Tyler's mother left their church which *"made them resistant to their [gay] son's declaration"* and that because her evangelical church taught her that homosexuality was a sin, she was negligent in preventing her son's apparent suffering.

The Huffington Post intellectualized how Christians today would comfortably engage in violent terrorism simply based on Christian views saying, stupidly, "Western Christianity was infected with imperial ideas, inflicted by the point of a sword, beginning in the ninth to 11th centuries.

These ideas sanctified violence and valorized killing for Christ as a means to hasten a new world order, and they endure in forms of contemporary Christianity, especially in white supremacist and Neo-Nazi movements."[111] *Salon* lamented in an article titled, *9 sinister things the Christian right does in the name of God,*: "...for Christians who are truly concerned about hostility toward their faith, I have a bit of advice: Don't be evil. And don't let your co-religionists get away with being evil either."[112]

A 2007 book titled *Kingdom Coming: The Rise of Christian Nationalism* is discussed in an interview with the author in which she demands that Christianity, "claims supernatural sanction for its campaign of national renewal and speaks rapturously about vanquishing the millions of Americans who would stand in its way."[113]

This is an ongoing narrative so deeply ingrained in our cultural mindset that within Christianity there has formed a liberal movement devoted to separating themselves from the ideas of 'hate' portrayed in mainstream Christianity. We see this in articles such as *The People Christians Are allowed to Hate* discussing why Christianity expressly forbids negative views of any living person the author writes: "There is no "except" or "unless" on the type of people Jesus commands us to love.

Not just Christians, not just people of your same ethnicity or socio-economic background, or sexual orientation. Everyone."[114] and *Why I Can't Say 'Love the Sinner/Hate the Sin' Anymore* where the author argues that "...despite all my theological disclaimers about how I'm just as much a sinner too, it's not the same. We don't use that phrase for everybody else. Only them. Only "the gays." That's the only place where we make "sinner" the all-encompassing identity."[115]

It would appear that entering a Christian house of worship would be similar to walking into a riot or a battlefield. The assumption being made demands that the unfamiliar visitor be wary and anticipate hostility. This past Sunday I had the opportunity to experience why everyone quoted above is simply wrong.

Upon invitation by a friend to see him preach at his church, I agreed and traveled to the service, and I can honestly say his sermon and his congregation provided a genuinely unique look into the everyday practices of Christian congregational expression.

The small country church in Kentucky is the picture-perfect setting to the above-mentioned authors. My friend who is a pastor there, greeted me as "Brother Chad" immediately with a smile and a strong handshake. He is aware I am gay and that I am Jewish. He did not hesitate in introducing me to his family who gregariously invited me to sit with them.

At this point it is relevant to point out that my personal friendship with this man does not cloud the experience but provides useful insight into it. If the above writers are correct and if he truly despised or feared me for being gay or Jewish, why would he sit me next to his wife?

Wearing a yarmulke, the rest of the congregation soon too became aware of my Jewish identity and yet despite this awareness insisted on shaking my hand and welcoming me to their spiritual home.

The service began with singing songs I was unfamiliar with but thematically revolved around a sense of personal exuberance in having found favor in the eyes of their savior. A lovely woman sang a song about personal triumph over life's difficulties that touched everyone in the room, myself included, and brought most to tears.

The sermon focused on his very personal struggles, salvation and the lessons he had learned when he chose to ignore the word of G-d in favor of his own ambitions. He credited his wife and the loving church community with bringing him to a place where he could recognize his own arrogance and agree to allow his faith to control his destiny.

The music, the community shouting out support and praise and the sermon connected this theme of recognizing the value of personal responsibility with the guidance of faith over humanity's desire to define and control every moment exclusively. Most importantly, from my objective perspective, the concept of failing G-d or sinning was shared rather than focused on anyone in particular.

The end of the service involved an emotional and fervent plea for anyone 'lost' or 'not saved' to come to the front to be prayed for. This plea lasted a long time and as the only stranger in the room it would not have been difficult to imagine it was for me alone, if I were looking for something to be offended by that is.

I twice thought I saw eyes looking at me or perhaps I felt them. As everyone left, I was invited back with happy smiles and handshakes from nearly everyone who attended. I could have chosen to have felt singled out and that is a large reason for this article.

The focus to abolish 'hate' by insisting Jesus exclusively demanded to love others or obsessively parsing every word of a sermon to find ignorance or intolerance assumes 'hate' is the motivation. The pastor, as well as likely every person in the room, felt a deep sense of personal connection and responsibility to G-d that they collectively agreed to keep each other honest with. The plea for salvation was for everyone.

This church and this service are unlikely to be an outlier of what normally goes on, but it is an indicator of what is experienced more widely. The attitude, the genuine community and the focus on personal responsibility to G-d are common in Christian churches. A strongly worded and passionate sermon, as the one I heard, is meant to inspire a sense of communal appreciation and caution of what lies outside of faith. Only if a person chooses to will they walk away believing it was all about them, although I understand each individual is meant to feel that in their own way.

How do I know they wouldn't have been hostile knowing I am gay since I didn't tell them? Well, that is kind of the point. It was simply not relevant. When a gay person describes hostility, they are often describing their own provocation of those around them and their interpretation of the response. Even when Christians call out to those, they consider lost in faith they do so with a tangible sense of love and compassion. The only way to be offended is if you choose to be.

Equal Violence,
Unequal Justice

September 18th, 2014 | Originally Published on American Thinker

OF THREE INNOCENT COUPLES violently attacked walking down the street in three cities in America in the last few weeks, one received more attention than the others. On August 25th 2014, a Jewish couple was attacked by Muslim men with pro-Palestinian flags in New York City. Two cars and several motorcycles surrounded the couple, and both were physically assaulted by the men.

They were believed to be stopped because the Jewish man was wearing a Yarmulke. On August 22nd 2014, a white couple was walking out of a night club in Missouri, close to the Ferguson riots, when a group of black men began harassing the girl. Caught on video, the men began to violently beat both the man and the woman.

On September 11th 2014, a gay couple was walking down the street in Pennsylvania when a group of white men and women surrounded them, reportedly shouted anti-gay slurs and began beating them. The attackers were captured on security footage before the attack. According to the gay victims, one was asked if he and the other young man were boyfriends. After saying yes, the group began calling them 'faggots' and began beating them. One of the victims kept screaming *"This is 2014, you can't do this!"* All media reports insist on describing the attackers as "well dressed, clean – cut white" individuals.[117,118]

A popular gay online magazine, *Queerty*, described this in their headline as a *"gang of violent heterosexuals."* This article describes a different beginning to the attack writing: "According to one of the victims, an assailant asked him if they were "fucking boyfriends," to which he replied, "yes, this is my fucking boyfriend." At this point, the assailant allegedly said "oh, so you're a dirty fag?" The victim says he responded to this with "yeah, maybe I am a dirty fag."[119] The attackers were also intoxicated. A quick Google news search reveals 12,100 news stories with multiple pages of identical headlines.

The attack on the white couple was largely only reported on Conservative websites. A Google news search reveals more than 7,000 stories but mixed results on the very first page. *The Huffington Post* does not appear to have a story on the incident after multiple searches, but a May 2014 article titled: "*Black-on-White Crime and the Reasons for a Media Double-Standard*" may provide some insight into that.

Lamenting a previous drudge headline about a black—on—white attack the author writes: "Every angry right-winger looking for an excuse for their ridiculous false equivalences about white racism versus "black racism" had a brand new hobby horse to ride." In regards to a white-on-black crime vs. a black-on-white crime detailed in the article he states: "They're different in terms of outcome, they're different in terms of details and each have very different historical and contemporaneous contexts."

He goes on to say "...there's a considerably wicked history in America of white racism, oppression and violence against black people, which, to an extent, continues today. It's the historical and contemporaneous context that ultimately changes how these stories are, and should be, covered." He asserts that when a white person kills a black person is it done from a "position of power" and the opposite is impossible to be considered equal since the minority cannot oppress the majority.

He concludes with this: "Yes, there's a double-standard. And until there's full equality and the long slow process of racial healing is completed, the double-standard has to remain."[120] The Jewish beating received exclusively Jewish newspaper mentions with less than five total news stories appearing in Google.

It appears that even though all the individuals are likely innocent, and all the groups involved in the beatings likely guilty, the value of the victims differ greatly. Instead of viewing each case as people being beaten in the open on the street, we are forced to focus on who did the beating and who was the victim in order to gauge our response. Each has a certain narrative value and can be used to advance the agenda of one group or another.

We ignore racism expressed by black people because liberalism must maintain a strict narrative that it does not exist. We must loudly proclaim from the rooftops that anti-gay violence is our nation's greatest threat because gay victimhood is more valuable than gay equality. Jews being attacked by Muslims over Israel is simply ignored as it does not help the Palestinian victim story.

Dozens of articles have been written reporting the frantic search for the 'well-dressed, clean-cut' white attackers including a large-scale twitter campaign to identify them through photos. A group picture reporting to show many of the victims has circulated throughout social media with close-ups of the attackers marked. Several suspects have been questioned by the police due to this aggressive search. The street camera caught the group walking before the event and from that footage they identified the suspects. The black suspects with similar video footage have yet to be found. No effort appears to be in effect to find the Muslim attackers in New York City at all.

It is reported that Pennsylvania does not currently cover hate crimes based on sexual orientation and so it is logical to expect a mighty push for this to be added to the legal system. The hate crime rate against gays is remarkably low at just 0.01% of the gay population. Of the 1,480 reported religious—based hate crimes in the United States in 2011, 63% were Jewish victims. Racially motivated crime is as such: 16% based on "anti—white" bias with 72% as "anti—black" bias, but race of the offender is not specified. There were 3,645 victims in 2011 in a country of 313 million people. Interestingly the FBI's *Hate Crimes* homepage features KKK members burning a large cross as its image.[38]

What does this tell us? It tells us that hate crimes are a remarkably low threat to any particular group within the United States. While some groups more openly verbalize bias crimes in various media than others, very few act upon the calls for violence for that motivation. What we see are isolated events supported or ignored solely based on their relevance to the media narrative. We do not need any grand social awakening or government intervention or investigations. If anything, the solution falls closer to home. If a person is concerned about being targeted, this ceases to be an issue if said person is capable of defending themselves.

Concealed carry, gun training, physical defense and rational situational awareness will protect more people than any hate crime law or campaign against 'hate' will. More importantly we will never appreciate equality if we, as a society, insist on magnifying only the incidents found to be useful to a particular and popular narrative. Mr. Cesca of the *Huffington Post* in the article referenced above is wrong. Racism, sexism or any bias towards another based on that person's perceived or actual association with a group is equally immoral.

No group deserves more or less sympathy, blame or protection and this is especially true when it happens to an innocent couple merely walking down the street anywhere in this country. While personal protection can save us individually, culturally we must stop picking and choosing who deserves attention and who does not.

Pro-Life is Pro-Choice

September 30th, 2014

FIGHTING LIBERAL MYTHOLOGY AND propaganda is incredibly difficult. People take a concept and mindlessly run with it until it is believed to be fact regardless of the evidence against it. As was explained in a recent Pro-Choice rant by feminist Amanda Marcotte: "Frankly, the more traditional, conservative argument against abortion—no, they're not going to lift a finger to help you with your unwanted baby and you should have thought about that before fucking, you stupid slut who deserves to suffer—at least has the refreshing scent of honesty to it."[121]

Liberalism has maintained for decades that conservatives are anti-poor because conservatives tend to vocally oppose liberal-inspired government support systems. To be more accurate, conservatives are anti-liberal policies. Liberal policies have only created a permanent poor class that continues to grow larger every year. Just as the image below displays a fundamental misunderstanding of how economics work:

Pro-choice supporters like Amanda Marcotte seem to be content with any argument that gives them the perception of winning; they aren't really thinking things through. The logical consequence of 'Pro-Birth *not* Pro-Life' is that poor people deserve to either be 100% cared for by the state or they will die. The poverty issue is fairly easy to combat because there is no other logical outcome than to demand a culling of poor people in order to reduce stress on the poor.

If we just killed every 5th poor person then the remaining poor would have more access to jobs, welfare resources, housing and medical care! Demanding that abortion positively impacts poverty is essentially that argument. It also defies reason that Pro-Life supporters would only care about birth. In some kind of reverse abortion logic, they seem to think Pro-Lifers think life stops as soon as the baby is born. That is ridiculous. The real issue for pro-choice advocates is that they are also liberals and think that if conservatives do not support *their* idea of social support through taxation, then they must default to not caring about the welfare of the child or family at all.

You see, in liberal utopia babies are born and immediately enter the state-approved welfare system where their food, housing, clothing, education and medical care are strictly regulated until they enter adulthood and then, they continue on in the same system. Liberals think of this as "compassion." Conservatives hate slavery and therefore oppose freedom-crushing taxation and the creation and maintenance of a dependent class who will never individually achieve more than what is allotted to them by the state.

Liberals think they are being clever by grabbing two entirely independent concepts and stitching them together to fabricate a conclusion, but in reality, they are merely displaying a remarkable misunderstanding of conservative policies and principles. Actually, it's not a misunderstanding as much as it is willful bigotry. They are not interested in any information that does not support their prejudice.

The meme of "Pro-Birth not Pro-Life" is a fantastic example of that. The shouting angry mob in the concept are projections of what liberals *think* conservatives are like but share absolutely nothing in common with actual conservatives. It displays a stereotype and is the result of prejudice and bigotry. The only thing they can do to support it is to demand that since conservatives do not support liberal welfare policies, it must be true. If conservatives supported liberal welfare policies, they would be liberals.

A more accurate approach would be to question why liberals cease to care about the welfare of the person or family *after* they are engaged in their support system. We have seen decades of social decline in the populations given the most support. Logically if the government supported the poorest population with housing, medical care, education, job training, food, counseling and on and on we should see the greatest achievements coming from that population. Not only should this group be healthier, better educated, more stable and creative, they should cease needing any assistance at all after just a few years.

Instead, we see continued high crime rates, health problems, poor education, no mobility and continued hunger from this group as evidenced by liberal demands for more and more programs and funding to quell the desperate need. Why don't they stop and ponder why this might be? Instead, they simply demand more money from the productive and use bully tactics to force it to happen. Liberals seem to believe poverty is static and must be merely maintained. Just like "unwanted pregnancy" they assume it simply is and therefore must be handled as a symptom.

They never look to the source. In fact, any attempts to look at the source results in violent outbursts of sexism and "slut shaming." We can't even approach the topic of why women, in an age with easy-to-access birth control for both sexes, abundant sexual education starting in elementary school and more opportunity for women to achieve any level of success in any field than at any time in the history of world, are still becoming pregnant when they are too young, too poor or not ready for the responsibility. The answer from the Left is: *More Money! More Education! More Government Provided Birth Control! And Easier, Faster Access to Abortion.*

Abortion is the only available solution to unwanted pregnancy liberal women find acceptable. Killing an innocent person is more of a viable solution than suggesting women take action to not get pregnant in the first place. Feminists frame this as sexism demanding we are punishing women for being sexually free and confident.

No. Women are not any more or any less capable of intelligent sexual choice than men are. In fact, our society strongly encourages women to consider their bodies as precious and to not be used by men who would not value them. This certainly originated in religious terms and has been and is in places around the world used to justify limiting women's freedom to choose any aspect of their lives, but in our time and in our country, it is literal.

Women can choose *not* to have sex. Women have rarely had this choice in human history.

Liberal feminists interpret this as a suggestion that women *should not* have sex. It actually is an affirmation that women are free to choose how, when and with whom to have sex. Just like our expectation that sexually active men are obligated to support both the woman and the child if pregnancy occurs as a consequence of his sexual choice, the woman also has responsibility. But even before the reality that creating an entirely new person is a responsibility and not an inconvenience, we have the basic understanding that a woman never has to be compelled into that position. If she has sex, it's because she chooses to (obviously excluding rape.)

Now, moving up a layer, women also have access to a variety of birth control options. Even with the sobbing hysteria over contraception, it is simply not an issue for a woman to obtain quality birth control that prevents ovulation. On top of that we have multiple physical options to prevent the mechanics from occurring and men are equally able to protect themselves. In our culture women are celebrated as being the sexually decisive ones as they agree to sexual advances from men. Even the most sexually aggressive women we see in our media are understood to be in charge and can change their minds at any time. If a man pushes past her "no" we have severe social and legal consequences.

A woman has a great deal of medical and social tools at her disposal to not get pregnant. This is not a stern disapproval of female sexual activity; it is an affirmation of female sexual empowerment. Women can decide all aspects of their sexuality and therefore they have absolute responsibility for their activity. This is the outcome of empowerment. When you have the power to decide you have the responsibility of your decision. This isn't an issue of "fault", it is a statement of rationality.

Liberals have a tendency to both declare female empowerment while simultaneously assuming female weakness. Women must be empowered to end their pregnancy but are too weak to prevent pregnancy from happening or too weak to continue on their empowered path with a child. Women are strong and powerful as single mothers but are too weak to build a life without direct support from the government. Women must be protected in order to prove they don't need protection. It's incredibly illogical.

No one is minimizing the impact of pregnancy. But to assume a woman's only choices are to hope she doesn't get pregnant and then fight endless poverty unless she either has copious government support or gets an abortion or to be a nun is mindbogglingly insulting. Pretending pregnancy is something similar to catching the flu is absurd and demonizing people who don't want to continue on eugenics by cleansing the poor population is illogical. Conservatives do not hate the poor; we just don't want them to remain poor. We know from decades of experience that liberal policies simply trap people into poverty and so we do not support further funding them. Abortion is a cruel and savage solution.

Conservatives want women, and men, to recognize that sexuality isn't a free-for-all experience. There are consequences because we are human. We can spread disease and sex is how we reproduce. It's not about punishment, it's about rational responsibility. No conservative wishes to remove any aspect that currently empowers women to fully control their sexuality and only conservatives support severe punishment for rapists. Conservatives want every person to make choices for themselves that better their lives and take responsibility for their actions. They don't want to damn people to a cycle of government dependence.

Do birth control methods fail? Yes. I am HIV+. If I do not take my medicine and my viral load increases and a man and I choose to have unprotected sex, there is a higher risk he will be infected. If I wear protection, there is still a chance. If I take my medication and my viral load decreases, then that chance is lessened. Sex is risky. Liberals want sex to not be risky.

They just declare that women should be able to have all the sex they want and never worry about consequences and then become morally offended when anyone points out that it's just a fantasy. When women do become pregnant in unprepared situations the men are held accountable financially regardless of their "choice" to be involved or not. Only women are celebrated for abandoning their responsibility in order to purse "their dreams."

Abortion is a symptom of liberalism. In our liberal society people grow up believing their needs should be cared for by others, their personal enjoyment is the single most important priority and regardless of their actions nothing is their fault. We see women who believe their immediate need is the only important priority and have no consideration for their or anybody else's life or future. In a world where they can make anything of their life and no one owns their body, they choose to be reckless and impulsive. Liberals seem offended that this would be a problem, but only in terms of women. Reckless, selfish and impulsive men are not protected.

But this post is about women's equality, true women's equality. Women have absolute control over their bodies and their sexuality. They have absolute reproductive freedom. They have every socially accepted platform available to be as sexual as they choose with zero harassment.

On top of that they live in the freest time they ever have in which they can literally achieve whatever they choose. Pregnancy isn't predictable, but it is extremely preventable. We need to stop treating women as though they are incapable of making good choices for themselves. Conservatives are Pro-Life because human life isn't inconvenient. We are pro-freedom because we want all people to have the freedom to choose their own path in life.

We are pro-responsibility because the second you give someone else power to own your mistakes you give them power to own your freedom. When women realize they can be confident, express their physical beauty, engage in any level or area of education, push forward into any career they choose and can experience sex 100% under their own decision, we will see less of a need for government to be there if they fall.

When women can see that sex is not compulsory or proof of their empowerment but is something directly connected to their own sense of well-being and part of their understanding of total personal care, then we won't need to demand government funded birth control and abortion.

When women realize that equality means the ability to build your own life without limitation from men, well they will become conservatives since Conservative Women already understand all of that right now. Liberalism limits women because they are women, Conservatism elevates women as people because they are people first.

Power to the People!...No Seriously

Ovtober 20th, 2014

Every election cycle I am forced to choose a candidate and a party I am not 100%, or even 70% behind in order to prevent the party I am 80-90% opposed to from gaining power. It's truly absurd. I vote Republican because there is no other viable choice.

I will typically always lean Republican because the last six years has shown me that Democrats are willing to absolutely sink the country, destroy Constitutional freedoms, impose taxes and laws onto the masses while openly giving special treatment to donors, special interest groups and big corporations, use the government to silence their opposition and lie with abandon because the media will never call them out for it. As I understand it, Democrats have always done this, but I have only been paying attention for about 10 years.

People I know who vote Democrat report doing so because they view Democrats as "trying to do something" to help people while Republicans merely say no and block their efforts. Republicans are viewed as the last remaining representatives of the old way of thinking. Also, Republicans are racists, sexists and homophobes and also crazy fascist Christians who want to outlaw scientific advances because the story of Noah doesn't mention any of it.

The problem is Republicans are fighting to stop Democrats and Democrats are fighting to keep their jobs at any cost and reshape the country to best benefit them. In the end, every couple of years we elect more or less of one and every 4 years we elect whoever is the opposite of who is currently President and who promises to undo everything said President has done. We are in a never-ending feud where we flip flop parties and never cease in being outraged over the results.

The real issue here is that we have given too much power to our government and the temporary person in power becomes more and more dramatically important to our individual experience. The government is expected to create jobs, shrink the debt, fight hate crimes, handle foreign affairs, regulate the environment, make sure education runs smoothly and on and on. Any change in ideology via the newest elected official means drastic change can occur with massive consequences.

Obama decided that the best way for all American's to experience health care was to require them by law to purchase insurance without the benefit of being able to influence the price in order to satisfy the liberal narrative of giving poor people "access" to health care. It didn't matter that the American people opposed it. It didn't matter that it was falsely described, implemented through unethical means and upheld by the Supreme Court as something it was not written into law to be.

The consequences of massive health care losses, insurance company panic and price raises, failed access to fulfill the law due to a website that won't work and financial destruction because no one will sign up for it and make the whole idea work do not deter the Democrats from pushing it forward. Their ideology blocks reason.

We never should have been in this position in the first place. What possible business does the government have in how people choose to pay for their health care? Insurance is a service purchased to cover medical costs just in case. Regardless of how difficult the medical business is – on a basic level the government should not be deciding what is best for all Americans in terms of purchasing a product for their personal needs.

But because we have a loud population that demands the government "give" them a livable wage, health care, protection from being offended and hundreds of other "benefits" we now fight over the extent of power the government has over our lives rather than realizing the government should never be involved.

If the government didn't micromanage us so closely the party in question would have less significance. We could go about our lives bickering over the details and basing our outrage over the larger world implications. Imagine the incredible absurdity of battling over the President of the United States to ensure you can receive birth control for free every month.

Unfortunately, we are going down such a bad path that I don't see it being fixed by a Republican president. The Democrats have realized they can get unregulated power without question, and they won't give that up. The more the government regulates "happiness" and "security" for our everyday lives the more power our elected officials have. Republicans typically stand for reducing that power. Many are realizing it benefits them more to go along with the Democrats.

Soon there will be barely any difference between them at all and they will have such a permanent majority that voting to limit terms or powers will be overwhelmed by their refusal to give up their own power. The smaller majority will lose their voice completely.

Liberals think this is wonderful because, currently, Democrats support their ideology. They think total domination is perfectly acceptable because their view is "correct" and therefore beneficial for everyone. If anyone disagrees, well too bad. They fail to recognize that ideology is temporary, and it can easily turn on them. Without a balanced option to combat it with new ideas everyone is trapped.

Liberals are bullies and think only in terms of what they want right now. Since it all works out on paper, they assume the future will be bright and wonderful. They simply do not understand that they are dooming themselves too. The 2012 election was our last chance to prevent Obamacare. It was a vital election because the outcome influenced so much. The 2014 mid-terms are vital because if we do not get a majority Republican/Conservative congress and Senate we will not be able to stop the rolling out of Obamacare permanently or prevent the numerous other actions liberal Democrats are forcing onto the country. 2016 will be pointless if we fail.

We should not be this close to the edge of radical change to our entire concept of freedom. We have precious few chances to get people into office who will curb the power abuse and that should be the focus. We need politicians who will pass term limits, power limits and define the court's authority. They must separate the Federal government from the States. They have to make sure that states have the ability to govern themselves. That is a tall order, and I don't know of any who can do it.

People who care about freedom have to be moved by politicians who declare they will limit the power and influence of their office and prevent any one group or organization from controlling the others. Their campaign platform must be to free Americans from burdensome taxation. Federal regulations and the threat of government retaliation via NSA spying, the IRS or other tools of intimidation.

We have to dismantle the monster and fix the debt before we can focus on social issues or fad political theater causes. If a politician promises to give you more jobs, raise your wages, and give you food, healthcare, housing etc. take it as a red flag. They want to control your life and make you dependent upon them.

The problem is our leaders have no incentive. We aren't rioting in the streets or surrounding their homes like in other places around the world so they know they can toss out a sound bite here or there and quell any uprising current. We shouldn't need to revolt. But we should use our influence while we have it. Why do liberals get their way? Because they badger politicians and businesses until they give in. Conservatives complain on the radio and blogs and hope politicians will listen and do the right thing.

Unfortunately, we lack a unified cause to do this. We aren't demanding the government serve us – we hope the government doesn't hurt us too badly or notice us. We don't need to riot in the streets, but why can't our politicians worry that their decisions, or lack thereof, will cause a flood of calls, donation withdraws and sponsoring of their competitors in the same category? If a business doesn't fulfill your needs, you demand a refund or go to another store. Why can't we do the same with our politicians?

Why the hell do we have Republicans in office for decades who do nothing but make us all angry at them for their appeasement of Democrats? Who keeps voting for these people? Just stop! If a judge votes down the voice of the people, why can't we impeach them or rally to vote them out of office? If your school board forces activities or bans activities that outrage your community – vote out the board! Get on the board yourself.

Liberals can shut down an entire school event over a prayer with a single outraged student protesting. Where are the hundreds of people who support the action? Why aren't they fighting back? When we rely on the government to fix things, we become sub-servant to them. We have the power right now to influence our local experience all the way to the state and that influences the federal government.

The problem is, I'm afraid, we will continue just as we are hoping it will get better and never find anything but more and more freedoms being removed from us. We wait for permission rather than taking action ourselves. We allow liberals to bully us and let the courts determine our fates. We have the power. We just aren't using it.

Do Not Feed the Animals

November 12th, 2014

Back in February President Obama continued the narrative that keeps the cycle of poverty going as described in Obama Weekly Address: *Give America A Raise*, "Hi, everybody. Restoring the idea of opportunity for all requires a year of action from all of us. Wherever I can act on my own, I will – and whenever I can ask more Americans to help, I'll do that too. In my State of the Union Address, for example, I asked more business leaders to take action to raise their employees' wages. Because even though our economy is growing, and our businesses have created about eight and a half million new jobs over the past four years, average wages have barely budged."[122]

In our arguing over concepts like the minimum wage, taxation and government entitlements we typically lump together "the poor" and make general emotional declarations over the impact any policy will have. Why do Democrat policies seem to impact people who are otherwise solidly conservative? I am in the working poor class where I qualify for government benefits but work 40+ hours per week above minimum wage.

I know many people who work extremely hard and are very dedicated to their jobs who barely scrape by on what they earn. They aren't buying cars and big screen TVs and they aren't demanding hand-outs either. They work to keep up with basic bills and necessities of life. I have talked about the obsession with blaming the rich for the problems of the poor and discussed how poor choices and a bad understanding of debt and money are mostly to blame.

This is a different perspective. Certainly, I personally do not utilize the money I earn to the most efficient way I could, and I waste a lot of it paying overdue bills and debts that I did not think through when I agreed to them. Credit cards, collections and other poor decisions have created a block of financial responsibility that I must take care of before I can begin moving towards the future. I own that. Many of us experience this. But what causes someone who works so incredibly hard at his job to barely be able to feed his kids?

The current Democrat and liberal answers are that he isn't paid enough and doesn't have access to enough social services. If he had healthcare, a higher minimum wage and benefits like food programs and other vouchers he would be able to live more freely. Previously the White House slammed the CBO's prediction that Despite common sense that says otherwise, Liberals insist the data proves both entitlements and the minimum wage do nothing but improve the lives of the poor.

But the "businesses deserve profit" argument also only exists in a conceptual argument. In real life, it doesn't help the worker to know his boss is getting rich off of his work. Liberals and Democrats often accuse Republicans of hating the poor as described by *dai lykos.com*, "Yes, because nothing makes a TeaBagger-Partyer happier and more giddy than to have hungry poor kids go without food and roughly 800,000 workers mosey along with no income. That should not surprise anyone since, after all, the GOP shutdown occurred because the Tea Party wanted to deny the working poor access to basic healthcare."[123]

This often expressed by conservatives opposing various Democrat proposed government programs which raise taxes on the productive. The Republican and conservative argument is that with nearly half the country being supported by the taxes of the other half the country is doomed to collapse. There is valid reasoning by generations of welfare recipients who never escape their monthly government check and never pay taxes into the system they are withdrawing from.

Even with this Democrats continue to introduce things like: *New Chance for a New Start in Life Act* which proposes to give grants to the unemployed for job training alongside increased unemployment benefits. And that is the key. The congresswoman proposing this, Sheila Jackson, states it perfectly: "For many Americans, this extension is a necessity of life."[124]

Democrats continuously demand, as did President Obama recently in his 2013 address: "Let's declare that in the wealthiest nation on Earth, no one who works full-time should have to live in poverty..."[125] that the problem is the outcome and the outcome is what must be addressed. Just like the legal requirement of all citizens to purchase health insurance with the promise of large subsidies for many to be covered by the same few who already support that same population through taxation does not "give poor people access to healthcare," raising the minimum wage hasn't created a boom of livable wealth to the poorest Americans. But what is appealing about this?

Why do people support this when it is so logically flawed? This is the same reasoning people who generally dislike the government and taxation are willing to work for the Federal or State government. Even though the general idea is a problem, the job itself pays great and gives great benefits which is more than can be often had in the private sector these days. Sure, unions are thugs and use intimidation techniques, but having an entire system designed to prevent you from being fired and ensuring high wages is pretty appealing.

This isn't a moral weakness. Its survival. Our grandparents earned a job and through loyalty and hard work continued getting paid more through promotions and their hard work and loyalty earned them a lifetime job. As long as they helped make their boss money, they were set. Others ventured into their own businesses and became wealthy while creating jobs for others. Its only when people began focusing on college as an intellectual journey, relied on a social safety net to get by and expected to work an entry-level job at ever-increasing wages and benefits that we began to see the downfall.

We go into debt before we even start job hunting and we have such a skewed via of work relations that we blame our employers for not paying us enough without ever factoring in our worth to the company or how we improve their business. We have so many people willing to not work and accept government assistance as "income" that people who really need it get caught in the masses. In fact, as *Forbes.com* reported, the White House itself feels this is a beneficial outcome: "…Secretary Jay Carney claimed that 2.5 million Americans leaving the workforce was a good thing, because they would no longer be "trapped in a job.""[126]

This is viewed as a progressively wonderful concept that people could work less hours, or not at all, and still be happily cared for by the government. The problem is that for millions of actually hard-working Americans, these proposals sound like they will directly benefit them in their everyday life. This was the appeal of the various bailouts and why people scramble for tax refunds every year. We have come to believe that wealth is out of our control.

But we have raised the minimum wage for decades and have a never-ending stream of government entitlements and yet we have an ever-growing population of people in need. By their logic, shouldn't this have been resolved by now?

The problem is that the hard-working people I know work for companies who are either too big to notice or are struggling to get by. They are forced to give a certain wage and a string of benefits, and their profit margin is smaller every year. Jason Furman, chairman of the Council of Economic Advisers, and Betsey Stevenson, Council of Economic Advisers member, wrote in a White House blog post "Opponents claim raising the minimum wage won't reduce poverty, but that is not the case, as many Americans who work full time are unable to make ends meet. This finding echoes the broad consensus of academic studies on the topic, which is nearly unanimous in finding that increases in the minimum wage reduce poverty,"

"Overall the logic for the finding that raising the minimum wage does not result in large adverse impacts on employment is that paying workers a better wage can improve productivity and thereby reduce unit labor costs. These adjustments, along with others that firms can make, help explain why the increase in the minimum wage need not lead to a reduction in employment. Higher wages lead to lower turnover, reducing the amount employers must spend recruiting and training new employees. Paying workers more can also improve motivation, morale, focus, and health, all of which can make workers more productive.

In addition, by reducing absenteeism, higher wages can increase the productivity of coworkers who depend on each other or work in teams. In addition, businesses can adjust in other ways rather than reducing employment (for example, by accepting lower profit margins). CBO's estimates do not appear to fully reflect the increased emphasis on all of these factors from the recent economics literature."[127]

Liberal logic continues to insist that what has failed so far must work if only in larger amounts and with more force. The end result of higher wages may be everything described above, but it fails to recognize where the wages come from in the first place. Sure, if my boss pays me $50 an hour, I will be happy, until he goes out of business. The whole point of starting a business is to make a profit. Accepting lower profit margins defeats the purpose of owning a business. We want workers to have ever increasing profits from working but we expect business owners to accept lower profits in order to provide that?

If a business must pay their employees more through wages and benefits despite their actual earnings, then they will have to make it up somehow. It is just assumed that the gap is in the "profit margin" but what if the company just doesn't sell enough to cover the mandatory costs imposed on them by the law?

The only option is they go out of business, and no one has a job. Also, when a person is being paid "minimum wage" their employer is not obligated to pay them anymore. It's a minimum. So, hard work, loyalty etc. do not equal higher wages. You could work at the same level for 5 years at the same wage and then the Minimum Wage rises, and someone gets hired a day later and you both get paid equally. Where is the incentive to work harder or be competitive?

Sure, many businesses paid their employees as little as possible and kept most of the profits in the past. Many businesses paid their employees well too. It was the employee's choice how much their work was worth, and you really tried to get a good job and keep it. Now people just want a job and are running out of options that don't trap them in the minimum wage cycle I just described. Unfortunately, Democrats and liberals are only focusing on the idea of the wage rather than the consequences.

They never consider the purpose of starting a business or what it takes to keep it afloat. The requirements to even consider hiring employees is simply not in the equation. Moreover, people demanding to be paid more because they feel they need more money to survive shows an incredible mass misunderstanding of how our economy even works. We seem to have come to a place where a job is viewed as a right.

The weight of regulations to improve the worker experience has, ironically, made it far more difficult to be one. You are under the mercy of a government decision in your industry rather than the effort of your own work. When prices no longer reflect the free market's will, the cost of living rises faster than wages rise. President Obama opining that wages have not risen in a year displays a misunderstanding of why wages should rise. It is unreasonable to measure wages across the board. Averaging the weight of Americans does not give insight into health. Each business is unique, and wages are meant to be competitive.

Unfortunately for the hard-working people I know personally, the market doesn't value what they offer. In an age of absolute equal experience, we are move comfortable with everyone earning just enough than we are with allowing individuals to succeed based on their work and effort. Businesses no longer have the freedom to reward their best workers because they have too many requirements to meet the needs their base workers. Debt continues to rise and more and more workers lose more and more of their checks through taxation. Anyone who looks at the deductions on their paystub understands how frustrating this is.

The problem is there is no solution and the appealing options of further government involvement in "securing" people's lives financially only puts us further into debt. Just as we can tell when tax refunds come every year that millions of Americans just scraping by don't get a boost and hold onto the funds for the rest of the year, we know that the solution is not giving more and more money or benefits. People have to earn their money to appreciate it. But earning money becomes harder every year.

The current system will collapse. The new generation of young adults in their 20's are all racking up huge student loan debts and credit card debt as we speak and have a President who casually tells them they don't have to work full time or even work at all and still deserve free healthcare and if they do work they deserve a minimum wage that is "livable." The generation that built social security through having their money taken for decades will now be expecting to use it in their old age and a sudden middle class of people in huge debt, middle-paying jobs and just out of reach of benefits will be paying for it all. That cannot continue on forever. The population getting will outnumber the population giving and it will collapse.

Perhaps that is what we need. Perhaps we need to climb out of the rubble and rebuild our lives freely. But until then people who believe they need the government to guide them throughout their lives will continue voting and supporting those who promise to give them more. And unfortunately, those who have a strong work ethic and are willing to support themselves are going to either realize their hard work is for nothing or will be forced into government dependence when they have no other options left.

Teach a Man to Fish

November 20th, 2014

Liberal thinking seems to be unable to distinguish between charity and forced taxation. A popular meme circulating the internet depicts a story of Jesus feeding the many in the Christian Bible that teaches a lesson about the abundance of G-d's love even in limited situations or times in our lives when things feel impossible. Jesus is described taking a small amount of food and turning it into more through a miracle that fed the entire population.

This story is also used as motivation and inspiration to gather food for the poor in various charity causes. The meme, however, uses this image to justify the government using taxes to feed the poor. The meme states: *"I can't feed these people, it will destroy their incentive to better themselves!"*

The meme is taking the logical reasoning used by conservatives in relation to government dependence and twisting it to appear as though they instead are willing to let people go hungry to prove a point. In Fiscal Year 2011, SNAP provided about $497.4 million dollars in food benefits to a monthly average of 345,955people in West Virginia. The population of WV in 2011 was roughly 1.8 million, nearly 20% of the state.

On a very basic level, a food assistance program is designed to temporarily help individuals and families supplement food needs during difficult times. Just like the Jesus story implies, the food provided was not infinite. The idea is that a person can have a safety net while they rebuild their lives from a struggle. The data shows a continual increase in those receiving benefits.

Food programs should reduce the number of people who need them. Liberal thinking celebrates this as an achievement for some reason and even attempts to spin it as a boost to the economy (see article connected to the image above) but the underlying issue is that the population requiring food stamps grows and the population receiving them do not pay taxes to help support it.

If your friend loses his job and you help him pay his bills until he gets a new job that is kindness and charity. If 3 years go by and you are still paying his bills that is dependence and both of you suffer. He is dependent upon you continuing to supply his needs and you are obligated to continue. If you stop – he has no other option. That is not kindness or charity. That is cruelty.

When a person depends on the state for their food, they never obtain any higher level than that. This is essentially like being in a zoo. You may be "secure" but you are dependent on someone else to feed you. The irony that the U.S. Government is very concerned about the possible harm dependency can have on wildlife if humans feed them. Why we believe this is not an issue for people is just illogical.

This argument is always framed as an issue of compassion. Liberals argue that limiting government programs is the result of conservative hatred of the poor. But they typically ignore why food prices rise, the debt of poor people and the constricting hold on business that prevents growth. Mandates like the Minimum Wage force people under a glass ceiling of potential earnings where they don't pay actual taxes (receiving tax refunds) and as a result fall into the category above. People skip meals or go without food because money management is no longer dependent on the Free Market and is more dependent on outside forces determining what is best. Dependency on a program funded through taxation is not a cure for this issue. It just grows the problem.

This is the fundamental flaw in the meme at the top of this post. Those who celebrate such an idea are actually missing the point. Charity that fills food banks, gives money to food organizations or participate in community gardens etc are efforts to help supplement gaps where they are needed. They are done out of love and kindness. They are volunteer efforts. People rarely live off of these efforts and very often join in them once they are better able to support themselves. The actions move forward and build on each other. That is what charity does.

Government programs funded through taxation are theft from working Americans for the benefit of supplying a lifestyle for non-working people, including non-citizens. People participating are given a credit card with a monthly balance to which they can purchase as much food as they want. This continues until they are no longer eligible. To maintain eligibility, they remain at the poverty level and simply accept the inflow of funds which support their lifestyle. Working people have no choice in supporting this and suffer the consequences of an imbalanced market which raises prices to compensate.

If government food programs supported positive outcomes by helping people get through difficult times until they could build a better life for themselves and begin contributing to the overall community, we would not see a continually growing need for the services. Jesus did not spend the rest of his life sitting in a tent with a fish and multiplying it every day to feed the masses of people.

The problem is the belief that government is required to keep people safe. The fact that people suffer is enough to demand government intervene. Instead of allowing the natural compassion and kindness shown in charity work as well as the human spirit to rise above to fix these situations – we use government theft from the productive to supply the lifestyle of the unproductive.

Those who are sick, elderly or who genuinely need assistance stand in longer and longer lines as those who could work choose to take the option of receiving rather than building for themselves. Food Stamp abuse is a serious issue as shown in this article: *Top 10 Reasons Food Stamps Need to Be Reformed:* "the amount of SNAP benefits paid in error is substantial, totaling about $2.2 billion in 2009."[128]

At the very core of the issue is the reality that like animals, people who become dependent on food programs are unable to fend for themselves. If a crash were to happen, eligibility standards changed or any kind of disaster occurred, these people are left unable to provide for themselves or their families. This is cruelty, not compassion.

We all suffer from dependence on convenience, but most of us know the value of our money and do our best to spend it wisely. Food purchases are done through careful needs-based assessments and pricing. If you were given $300 a month to buy food with and it was always going to be there you would care less about how much things cost. Just like "free" healthcare results in back-end costs being less important. If a medical option costs $10 or $1000 it doesn't matter to you if you never pay for it directly. This is the same with food purchasing. Food programs do not reduce hunger, they take money from some people and give it to others. People who participate do not benefit; they just get free money.

Conservatives, religiously devoted people and average people are compassionate and giving and care for those in need through a wide variety of charity options. To say conservatives hate the poor or want people starving is simply bigotry since it is overwhelmingly untrue. Conservatives hate the enslavement that government dependence creates, and they do not want to end up like Greece or the European Union whose entitlement programs crushed the economy. Conservatives don't want people to lower their own potential by relying on the government to supply their entire lifestyle from birth to death with program after program.

Liberals care about the poor too, obviously, but seem to be willing to ignore decades of evidence that their ideas only harm in the short and long term. They focus on government requirements and equality through force, and it always ends up with people limiting their own potential. Free Markets and capitalism allow a person from any level of life to rise to any level they can possibly achieve.

This is done through their work alone. Without crushing government regulation, laws and other enforcement meant to force a concept of equality, they thrive and spread the wealth naturally. With crushing government regulation, laws and other enforcement meant to force a concept of equality, masses stay at the same level indefinitely and never rise higher than they are allowed.

We no longer know how to grow food, gather food, hunt food, prepare food etc. like our ancestors did. My great-grandmother gathered greens from the woods when her family had no money for food. She knew how to do this. Most of us would starve without access to a grocery store and a working stove. We have become dependent ourselves. The problem is not that people should be expected to take care of themselves, the problem is that the more freedom we give to another authority, the less we have for ourselves if we ever choose to be more than we are now.

Participating in food programs is not shameful any more than accepting charity when you need it. We should not view it as a lifelong lifestyle option. Those who oppose further government spending on entitlement programs are doing so because they know the destructive consequences it brings. With we cannot survive with an ever growing population entirely dependent on tax-funded programs to support them.[129]

References

1 Jeltsen, Melissa (2012) 'Dan Savage Reacts To Gay Conservative Group Endorsing Romney With Explicit Tweet | HuffPost Voices'. *Huffington Post.* [online] Available from: https://www.huffpost.com/entry/dan-savage-reacts-to-gay_n_1613831 (Accessed 30 January 2023)

2 Ruse, Austin (2014) 'Making Your Way Through Facebook's 58 Genders'. *Breitbart.* [online] Available from: https://www.breitbart.com/politics/2014/02/21/making-your-way-through-facebook-58-genders/ (Accessed 30 January 2023)

3 Davis, Troy (2011) 'Why Chaz Bono Is a Misogynist Who Does Not Represent Us | Super-Mattachine'. *Super Mattachine Review.* [online] Available from: https://supermattachine.wordpress.com/2011/09/19/why-chaz-bono-is-a-misogynist-who-does-not-represent-us/ (Accessed 30 January 2023)

4 McDonald, Soraya Nadia (2014) 'Seven questions about transgender issues you were afraid to ask'. *Washington Post.*

5 Keefe, Valerie (2012) 'Trans 101: A Primer for the Ignorant and the Intolerant | HuffPost Voices'. *Huffington Post.* [online] Available from: https://www.huffpost.com/entry/trans-101_b_1198674 (Accessed 30 January 2023)

6 Keefe, Valerie (2011) 'Pardon Andrea Jones | HuffPost Voices'. *Huffington Post.* [online] Available from: https://www.huffpost.com/entry/pardon-andrea-jones_b_1098889 (Accessed 30 January 2023)

7 Ford, Zack (2014) 'Janet Mock Schools Piers Morgan On How To Tell Transgender Stories – ThinkProgress'. *ThinkProgress.* [online] Available from: https://archive.thinkprogress.org/janet-mock-schools-piers-morgan-on-how-to-tell-transgender-stories-f5086f1934ff/ (Accessed 30 January 2023)

8 Kirell, Andrew (2012) 'Fordham University President Scolds College Republicans For Booking Ann Coulter, "Repugnant" Speech'. *Mediaite.* [online] Available

from: https://www.mediaite.com/online/fordham-university-president-scorns-college
-republicans-for-booking-ann-coulters-repugnant-speech/ (Accessed 30 January 2023)

9 Re, Gregg (2012) 'Campus president condemns Coulter event, silent as professor
who calls sex with animals potentially "satisfying" speaks | The Daily Caller'. *Daily Caller*.
[online] Available from: https://dailycaller.com/2012/11/17/after-barring-ann-coul
ter-from-campus-fordham-university-welcomes-infanticide-advocate-peter-singer/ (Accessed 30 January 2023)

10 Sheppard, Noel (2012) 'Jane Fonda and Gloria Steinem Call for FCC
to Ban Rush Limbaugh | Newsbusters'. *MRC NewsBusters*. [online] Available
from: https://www.newsbusters.org/blogs/nb/noel-sheppard/2012/03/10/jane-fonda
-and-gloria-steinem-call-fcc-ban-rush-limbaugh (Accessed 30 January 2023)

11 Urbanski, Dave (2014) 'Star Trek' Actor Promises Trouble for Arizona If Gov.
Signs What He Calls "Turn Away the Gay" Bill - TheBlaze'. *The Blaze*. [online] Available from: https://www.theblaze.com/news/2014/02/22/star-trek-actor-promises-tro
uble-for-arizona-if-gov-signs-what-he-calls-turn-away-the-gay-bill (Accessed 30 January
2023)

12 Zazzle (n.d.) 'What Content is Acceptable for Designs on Zazzle? – Zazzle Help
Center'. [online] Available from: https://help.zazzle.com/hc/en-us/articles/21914434
8-What-Content-is-Acceptable-for-Designs-on-Zazzle-] (Accessed 30 January 2023)

13 Hawkins, Awr (2014) 'Florida Lawmakers Push "Toaster Pastry Gun Freedom
Act"'. *Breitbart*. [online] Available from: https://www.breitbart.com/politics/2014
/01/30/florida-lawmakers-push-toaster-pastry-gun-freedom-act/ (Accessed 30 January
2023)

14 Pollak, Joel B. (2014) 'Blue State Blues: The Gay Intolerance Act of 2014'. *Breitbart*.
[online] Available from: https://www.breitbart.com/politics/2014/02/28/blue-state-b
lues-the-gay-intolerance-act-of-2014/ (Accessed 31 January 2023)

15 Mehta, Hemant (2013) 'Anti-Gay Christian Leader Whines About How Gay Couples Want Equal Treatment at Christian-Owned Businesses'. *OnlySky*. [online] Available from: https://onlysky.media/hemant-mehta/anti-gay-christian-leader-whines-abo
ut-how-gay-couples-want-equal-treatment-at-christian-owned-businesses/ (Accessed 31
January 2023)

16 Ritz, Erica (2013) 'Oregon Baker Faces State Investigation After Refusing to Make
Same-Sex Couple's Wedding Cake - TheBlaze'. *The Blaze*. [online] Available from:
https://www.theblaze.com/news/2013/02/02/baker-under-investigation-after-declinin

g-to-make-gay-couples-wedding-cake-if-i-have-to-be-penalized-for-my-beliefs-so-be-it (Accessed 31 January 2023)

17 Canaday, Margot (2008) 'We Colonials: Sodomy Laws in America | The Nation'. *The Nation*. [online] Available from: https://www.thenation.com/article/archive/we-colonials-sodomy-laws-america/ (Accessed 31 January 2023)

18 Sieczkowski, Cavan (2013) 'New Jersey Waitress In Anti-Gay Receipt Saga Reportedly Let Go From Job | HuffPost Voices'. *Huffington Post*. [online] Available from: https://www.huffpost.com/entry/new-jersey-waitress-let-go-anti-gay_n_4412028 (Accessed 31 January 2023)

19 Rogers (2014) 'HB 1547'. *Tennessee Senate*. [online] Available from: https://www.capitol.tn.gov/Bills/108/Bill/HB1547.pdf (Accessed 31 January 2023)

20 Brown, Richard C. (2014) 'Tennessee Bill Passes That Will Allow The Bullying Of LGBT Students in the Name Of "Religious Freedom"'. *Back2Stonewall*. [online] Available from: http://www.back2stonewall.com/2014/03/tennessee-bill-passes-bullying-lgbt-students-religious-freedom.html (Accessed 31 January 2023)

21 Sankin, Aaron (2012) 'Abortion Poverty Study Finds Link Between Lack Of Access And Income | HuffPost San Francisco'. *Huffington Post*. [online] Available from: https://www.huffpost.com/entry/abortion-poverty-study_n_2130890 (Accessed 31 January 2023)

22 Arthur, Joyce (2001) 'THE PRO-CHOICE ACTION NETWORK'. *Pro Choice Action Network*. [online] Available from: https://www.prochoiceactionnetwork-canada.org/articles/fetusperson.shtml (Accessed 31 January 2023)

23 LifeSite (2014) 'Obama celebrates Roe v. Wade's 41st anniversary: abortion allows women to "fulfill their dreams" - LifeSite'. *LifeSite News*. [online] Available from: https://www.lifesitenews.com/news/obama-celebrates-roe-v.-wades-41st-anniversary-abortion-allows-women-to-ful/ (Accessed 31 January 2023)

24 Greene, Chad Felix (2014) 'Gay Rights: An Unnecessary Battle - American Thinker'. *American Thinker*. [online] Available from: https://www.americanthinker.com/articles/2014/04/gay_rights_an_unnecessary_battle.html (Accessed 31 January 2023)

25 Terkel, Amanda (2014) 'Georgia, Mississippi Backtrack On Bills Mirroring Arizona Anti-Gay Legislation | HuffPost Latest News'. *Huffington Post*. [online] Available from: https://www.huffpost.com/entry/anti-gay-bills_n_4868169 (Accessed 31 January 2023)

26 Greene, Chad Felix (2014) 'Pro-Choice: Defending the Right Not to be Gay - American Thinker'. *American Thinker.* [online] Available from: https://www.americanthinker.com/articles/2014/04/prochoice_defending_the_right_not_to_be_gay.html (Accessed 31 January 2023)

27 Anon (2012) 'Bill Text - SB-1172 Sexual orientation change efforts.' *California Legislature.* [online] Available from: https://leginfo.legislature.ca.gov/faces/billNavCl ient.xhtml?bill_id=201120120SB1172 (Accessed 31 January 2023)

28 Benkof, David (2014) 'Nobody is "born that way," gay historians say | The Daily Caller'. *Daily Caller.* [online] Available from: https://dailycaller.com/2014/03/19/no body-is-born-that-way-gay-historians-say/ (Accessed 31 January 2023)

29 Greene, Chad Felix (2014) 'Conservatism: The Best Choice a Gay Person Can Make - American Thinker'. *American Thinker.* [online] Available from: https://www.americanthinker.com/articles/2014/04/conservatism_the_best_ch oice_a_gay_person_can_make.html (Accessed 31 January 2023)

30 Ellis, Blake (2012) 'Gay people earn more, owe less'. *CNN Money.* [online] Available from: https://money.cnn.com/2012/12/06/pf/gay-money/ (Accessed 31 January 2023)

31 Gates, Gary J. and Newport, Frank (2012) 'Special Report: 3.4% of U.S. Adults Identify as LGBT'. *Gallup.* [online] Available from: https://news.gallup.com/poll/158 066/special-report-adults-identify-lgbt.aspx (Accessed 31 January 2023)

32 Stern, Mark Joseph (2013) 'Are gay people smarter than straight people, or do they just work harder?' *Slate.* [online] Available from: https://slate.com/human-interest/2013/09/are-gay-people-smarter-than-straigh t-people-or-do-they-just-work-harder.html (Accessed 31 January 2023)

33 Salam, Reihan (2014) 'Tax credits and children: Parents should pay lower taxes, and childless people should pay higher taxes.' *Slate.* [online] Available from: https://slate.com/news-and-politics/2014/03/tax-credits-and-children-parents-s hould-pay-lower-taxes-and-childless-people-should-pay-higher-taxes.html (Accessed 31 January 2023)

34 Experian (2013) 'What the DOMA and Prop8 rulings mean for marketers - Marketing Forward Blog'. *Experian.* [online] Available from: https://www.experian.com/blogs/marketing-forward/2013/06/27/what-the-do ma-and-prop8-rulings-mean-for-marketers/ (Accessed 19 August 2020)

35 Bradley, Tony (2014) 'Backlash Against Brendan Eich Crossed A Line'. *Forbes*. [online] Available from: https://www.forbes.com/sites/tonybradley/2014/04/05/back lash-against-brendan-eich-crossed-a-line/?sh=2d0863f26f8a (Accessed 31 January 2023)

36 Greene, Chad Felix (2014) 'The True Legacy of Matthew Shepard - American Thinker'. *American Thinker*. [online] Available from: https://www.americanthinker.com/articles/2014/04/the_true_legacy_of_matthew_shepard.html (Accessed 31 January 2023)

37 Mathew's Place (2013) 'Mathew Shepard 2013 Annual Report'. *Matthew Shepard Foundation*. [online] Available from: http://fab5d476195e492b8fe8-8aba12ac57cbd7bc843c664b09bb2eac.r60.cf1.rackcdn.com/wp-content/uploads/MSF_AR_2014Revised-1.pdf (Accessed 31 January 2023)

38 FBI (n.d.) 'FBI — Hate Crime'. *UCR.FBI.GOV*. [online] Available from: https://ucr.fbi.gov/hate-crime (Accessed 20 August 2020)

39 Tzatzev, Aleksi (2012) 'Anti-Gay Hate Crime Stats Don't Budge'. *Insider*. [online] Available from: https://www.businessinsider.com/anti-gay-hate-crime-stats-dont-budge-2012-12 (Accessed 31 January 2023)

40 UCLA (2015) 'Intimate Partner Violence and Sexual Abuse Among LGBT People – Williams Institute'. *UCLA School of Law Williams Institute*. [online] Available from: https://williamsinstitute.law.ucla.edu/publications/ipv-sex-abuse-lgbt-people/ (Accessed 18 August 2020)

41 CDC (2017) 'HIV and Gay and Bisexual Men | HIV by Group | HIV/AIDS | CDC'. *Centers for Disease Control and Prevention*. [online] Available from: https://www.cdc.gov/hiv/group/msm/index.html (Accessed 18 August 2020)

42 Hicklin, Aaron (2013) 'Have We Got Matthew Shepard All Wrong?' *The Advocate*. [online] Available from: https://www.advocate.com/print-issue/current-issue/2013/09/13/have-we-got-matthew-shepard-all-wrong?page=full (Accessed 17 August 2020)

43 Anon (n.d.) 'Anti-abortion violence - Wikipedia'. [online] Available from: https://en.wikipedia.org/wiki/Anti-abortion_violence (Accessed 31 January 2023)

44 Freeman, Tzvi (n.d.) 'Why Get Married? - Is marriage worth the sacrifice? - Chabad.org'. *Chadbad.org*. [online] Available from: https://www.chabad.org/library/article_cdo/aid/482475/jewish/Why-Get-Married.htm (Accessed 31 January 2023)

45 Greene, Chad Felix (2014) 'Michael Sam: A Fictional Victory? - American Thinker'. *American Thinker*. [online] Available from: https://www.americanthinker.com/articles/2014/05/michael_sam_a_fictional_victory.html (Accessed 31 January 2023)

46 Carter, Chelsea J. and Ellis, Ralph (2014) 'Obama congratulates Michael Sam, first openly gay NFL draftee - CNN'. *CNN*. [online] Available from: https://www.cnn.com/2014/05/10/us/football-michael-sam/] (Accessed 31 January 2023)

47 Obama, Michelle (2014) 'First Lady- Archived on Twitter: "You're an inspiration to all of us, @MikeSamFootball. We couldn't be prouder of your courage both on and off the field. -mo" / Twitter'. *Twitter*. [online] Available from: https://twitter.com/FLOTUS44/status/432896998279495680 (Accessed 31 January 2023)

48 Sports Center (2014) 'SportsCenter on Twitter: "NFL statement: 'We admire Michael Sam's honesty and courage. We look forward to welcoming and supporting Michael Sam in 2014.'" / Twitter'. *Twitter*. [online] Available from: https://twitter.com/SportsCenter/status/432688447539527680 (Accessed 31 January 2023)

49 Anon (n.d.) 'White privilege - Wikipedia'. [online] Available from: https://en.wikipedia.org/wiki/White_privilege (Accessed 31 January 2023)

50 Greene, Chad Felix (2014) 'Rational Christianity: the Benham Brothers - American Thinker'. *American Thinker*. [online] Available from: https://www.americanthinker.com/articles/2014/05/rational_christianity_the_benham_brothers.html (Accessed 31 January 2023)

51 Hafiz, Yasmine (2014) 'Christian Activists Rally Behind Benham Brothers Following Cancellation Of HGTV Show | HuffPost Religion'. *Huffington Post*. [online] Available from: https://www.huffpost.com/entry/christian-activists-benham-brothers-hgtv_n_5289625 (Accessed 31 January 2023)

52 Anon (2014) 'HGTV Drops Benham Brothers' "Flip It Forward" After Anti-Gay Views Are Unearthed | HuffPost Voices'. *Huffington Post*. [online] Available from: https://www.huffpost.com/entry/hgtv-benham-brothers-anti-gay_n_5287322 (Accessed 31 January 2023)

53 Tashman, Brian (2014) 'HGTV Picks Anti-Gay, Anti-Choice Extremist For New Reality TV Show | Right Wing Watch'. *Right Wing Watch*. [online] Available from: https://www.rightwingwatch.org/post/hgtv-picks-anti-gay-anti-choice-extremist-for-new-reality-tv-show/ (Accessed 31 January 2023)

54 Nolte, John (2014) 'Christian Hosts Lose HGTV Show For Opposing Homosexuality, Abortion'. *Breitbart*. [online] Available

from: https://www.breitbart.com/entertainment/2014/05/07/christian-host-lose-hgtv-show-for-opposing-homosexuality-abortion/ (Accessed 31 January 2023)

55 Hallowell, Billy (2014) 'Christian Brothers Whose HGTV Show Was Canceled Over Their Views on Homosexuality and Abortion Respond in a Surprising Way - TheBlaze'. *The Blaze*. [online] Available from: https://www.theblaze.com/news/2014/05/09/christian-brothers-whose-hgtv-was-canceled-over-their-views-on-homosexuality-and-abortion-respond-in-a-surprising-way (Accessed 31 January 2023)

56 LaSalvia, Jimmy (2014) 'Consequences'. *jimmylasalvia.com.*

57 Greene, Chad Felix (2014) 'Transphobia: A Reasonable Response? - American Thinker'. *American Thinker*. [online] Available from: https://www.americanthinker.com/articles/2014/05/transphobia_a_reasonable_response.html (Accessed 31 January 2023)

58 Beredjick, Camille (2012) 'DSM Replaces Gender Identity Disorder With Gender Dysphoria'. *Advocate*. [online] Available from: https://www.advocate.com/politics/transgender/2012/07/23/dsm-replaces-gender-identity-disorder-gender-dysphoria (Accessed 31 January 2023)

59 Aetna (n.d.) 'Gender Affirming Surgery - Medical Clinical Policy Bulletins | Aetna'. [online] Available from: http://www.aetna.com/cpb/medical/data/600_699/0615.html (Accessed 31 January 2023)

60 Athem Blue Cross (n.d.) 'Clinical Indications for Gender Reassignment Surgery'. [online] Available from: https://studenthealth.ucsf.edu/sites/studenthealth.ucsf.edu/files/PDF/Gender%20Reassignment%20Surgery_Anthem_new.pdf (Accessed 31 January 2023)

61 Grant, Jaime M, Mottet, Lisa A, Justin Tanis, JD, with Jack Harrison Jody Herman, DMin L and Keisling, Mara (2012) 'Injustice at Every Turn A Report of the National Transgender Discrimination Survey'. *Trans Equality*.

62 Greene, Chad Felix (2014) '#YesAllNormal: Standing up for the Average Man - American Thinker'. *American Thinker*. [online] Available from: https://www.americanthinker.com/articles/2014/06/yesallnormal_standing_up_for_the_average_man.html (Accessed 31 January 2023)

63 Anon (2011) 'FBI — Expanded Homicide Data'. [online] Available from: https://ucr.fbi.gov/crime-in-the-u.s/2011/crime-in-the-u.s.-2011/offenses-known-to-law-enforcement/expanded/expanded-homicide-data (Accessed 31 January 2023)

64 Cooper, Brittney (2014) 'White guy killer syndrome: Elliot Rodger's deadly, privileged rage | Salon.com'. *Salon*. [online] Available from: https://www.salon.com/2014/05/27/white_guy_killer_syndrome_elliot_rodgers_deadly_privileged_rage/ (Accessed 31 January 2023)

65 Marcotte, Amanda (2014) 'Campus sexual assault statistics: So many victims, but not as many predators.' *Slate*. [online] Available from: https://slate.com/human-interest/2014/05/campus-sexual-assault-statistics-so-many-victims-but-not-as-many-predators.html (Accessed 31 January 2023)

66 P, Doug (2014) '"Perfect example of male entitlement": Pro-feminist supporters of #YesAllWomen angry about #YesAllPeople – twitchy.com'. *Twitchy*. [online] Available from: https://twitchy.com/2014/05/25/perfect-example-of-male-entitlement-pro-feminist-supporters-of-yesallwomen-angry-about-yesallpeople/ (Accessed 31 January 2023)

67 Broderick, Ryan, Nigatu, Heben and Testa, Jessica (2014) 'What Is Rape Culture?' *Buzzfeed News*. [online] Available from: https://www.buzzfeednews.com/article/ryanhatesthis/what-is-rape-culture (Accessed 31 January 2023)

68 Wolf, Naomi, Bindel, Julie, Power, Nina, Gupta, Rahila, et al. (2012) 'Sexism and misogyny: what's the difference?' *The Guardian*. [online] Available from: https://www.theguardian.com/commentisfree/2012/oct/17/difference-between-sexism-and-misogyny (Accessed 31 January 2023)

69 Lewis, Matt K. (2015) 'In defense of old white men | The Week'. *The Week*. [online] Available from: https://theweek.com/articles/446515/defense-old-white-men#axzz33Cz0Vur3 (Accessed 31 January 2023)

70 Coulter, Ann (2014) 'Lockett & Load'. *Anncoulter.com*. [online] Available from: https://anncoulter.com/2014/05/07/lockett-load/ (Accessed 31 January 2023)

71 Livingston, Gretchen (2013) 'The Rise of Single Fathers | Pew Research Center'. *Pew Research Center*. [online] Available from: https://www.pewresearch.org/social-trends/2013/07/02/the-rise-of-single-fathers/ (Accessed 31 January 2023)

72 Greene, Chad Felix (2014) 'Conservative Feminism: Truly Empowering Women - American Thinker'. *American Thinker*. [online] Available from: https://www.americanthinker.com/articles/2014/06/conservative_feminism_truly_empowering_women.html (Accessed 31 January 2023)

73 Ziganto, Lori (2014) 'Fight like a girl! Katie Pavlich has a question for "self-defense is icky" Cosmo editor – twitchy.com'. *Twitchy*. [online] Available

from: https://twitchy.com/2014/06/09/fight-like-a-girl-katie-pavlich-has-a-question-for-self-defense-is-icky-cosmo-editor/ (Accessed 31 January 2023)

74 Ziganto, Lori (2014) 'How does a HuffPo editor's idiocy expose "everything wrong with feminism in a single tweet"? Like this – twitchy.com'. *Twitchy*. [online] Available from: https://twitchy.com/2014/06/09/how-does-a-huffpo-editors-idiocy-expose-everything-wrong-with-feminism-in-a-single-tweet-like-this/ (Accessed 31 January 2023)

75 Zerlina (2013) 'Telling women to get a gun is not rape prevention'. *Feministing*. [online] Available from: http://feministing.com/2013/03/07/telling-women-to-get-a-gun-is-not-rape-prevention/ (Accessed 31 January 2023)

76 Mariotte, David W. (2013) 'Chivalry degrades women, promotes sexism in society - The Daily Wildcat'. *The Daily Wildcat*. [online] Available from: https://www.wildcat.arizona.edu/article/2013/10/chivalry-degrades-women-promotes-sexism-in-society (Accessed 31 January 2023)

77 Palvich, Katie (2014) 'Part 1: A Conversation With World Shooting Champion Julie Golob'. *Townhall*. [online] Available from: https://townhall.com/columnists/katiepavlich/2014/01/20/part-1-a-conversation-with-world-shooting-champion-julie-golob-n1781426 (Accessed 31 January 2023)

78 Nussbaum, Daniel (2014) 'CA Bill Demands Verbal or Written Consent for Sex on College Campuses'. *Breitbart*. [online] Available from: https://www.breitbart.com/local/2014/06/04/college-students-may-need-verbal-or-written-consent-to-have-sex-on-campus/ (Accessed 31 January 2023)

79 Anon (2013) '5 Ways We Can Teach Men Not to Rape'. *Ebony*. [online] Available from: https://www.ebony.com/5-ways-we-can-teach-men-not-to-rape-456/#axzz34AutiO7X (Accessed 31 January 2023)

80 Greene, Chad Felix (2014) 'Liberal Sex Ed and Rational Opposition - American Thinker'. *American Thinker*. [online] Available from: https://www.americanthinker.com/articles/2014/06/liberal_sex_ed_and_rational_opposition.html (Accessed 31 January 2023)

81 Culp-Ressler, Tara (2013) 'As Chicago Kids Head Back To School, Conservatives Freak Out About "Kindergarten Sex Ed" '. *ThinkProgress*.

82 Huston, Matt (2012) 'Is Your Child's Sexual Behavior Normal? | Psychology Today'. *Psychology Today*. [online] Available from: https://www.psychologytoday.com/intl/blog/stop-the-cycle/201201/is-your-child-s-sexual-behavior-normal (Accessed 31 January 2023)

83 Anon (n.d.) 'Pedophilia | Psychology Today'. [online] Available from: https://www.psychologytoday.com/intl/conditions/pedophilia (Accessed 31 January 2023)

84 @fakedansavage (2014) 'Dan Savage - Twitter'. *Twitter*.

85 Caprara, Collette (2011) 'Teen Sexual Behavior: Promoting Wise Choices'. *The Daily Signal*. [online] Available from: https://www.dailysignal.com/2011/10/13/teen-sexual-behavior-promoting-wise-choices/ (Accessed 31 January 2023)

86 Ryan, Christopher (2013) 'Can Pedophilia Ever Be "Mild"? | Psychology Today'. *Psychology Today*. [online] Available from: https://www.psychologytoday.com/intl/blog/sex-dawn/201309/can-pedophilia-ever-be-mild (Accessed 31 January 2023)

87 Greene, Chad Felix (2014) 'Uganda, Anti-Gay Laws, and Liberalism - American Thinker'. *American Thinker*. [online] Available from: https://www.americanthinker.com/articles/2014/06/6_22_2014_14_5.html (Accessed 31 January 2023)

88 BBC News (2014) 'US imposes sanctions on Uganda for anti-gay law - BBC News'. *BBC News*. [online] Available from: https://www.bbc.com/news/world-us-canada-27933051 (Accessed 31 January 2023)

89 Gjorgievska, Aleksandra (2014) 'U.S. Unveils Measures Against Uganda's Anti-Homosexuality Law | Time'. *Time*. [online] Available from: https://time.com/2902234/us-uganda-homosexuality/ (Accessed 31 January 2023)

90 Shukla, Suhag A. (2014) 'Uganda's Anti-Gay Law and America's Right Hand | HuffPost Religion'. *Huffington Post*. [online] Available from: https://www.huffpost.com/entry/ugandas-anti-gay-law-and_b_5516498 (Accessed 31 January 2023)

91 Kumar, Anugrah (2014) 'Rick Warren Squashes Rumors; Says He Strongly Opposes Uganda's Anti-Homosexuality Law | U.S. News'. *Christian Post*. [online] Available from: https://www.christianpost.com/news/rick-warren-responds-to-rumors-says-he-strongly-opposes-ugandas-anti-homosexuality-law-115483/ (Accessed 31 January 2023)

92 Parsons, Christi (2014) 'White House: Obama to sign order banning anti-gay discrimination - Los Angeles Times'. *Los Angeles Times*. [online] Available from: https://www.latimes.com/nation/politics/politicsnow/la-na-nn-obama-gay-rights-20140616-story.html (Accessed 31 January 2023)

93 Robles, Frances (2014) 'Fleeing Gangs, Children Head to U.S. Border'. *The New York Times*, 8th July.

94 Anon (2014) 'Desperate Journey: Crime and Poverty Drive Honduran Kids to U.S.' *NBC News*. [online] Available

from: https://www.nbcnews.com/storyline/immigration-border-crisis/desperate-journey-crime-poverty-drive-honduran-kids-u-s-n150011 (Accessed 31 January 2023)

95 Grim, Ryan and Bendery, Jennifer (2014) 'Shocking Photos Of Humanitarian Crisis On U.S. Border Emerge | HuffPost Latest News'. *Huffington Post*. [online] Available from: https://www.huffpost.com/entry/border-patrol-children_n_5462054 (Accessed 31 January 2023)

96 Jones, Kara (2014) 'U.N. Pushes U.S. to Call Illegal Immigrants "Refugees"'. *Townhall*. [online] Available from: https://townhall.com/tipsheet/karajones/2014/07/08/un-pushes-us-to-call-illegal-immigrants-refugees-n1860122 (Accessed 31 January 2023)

97 Luhnow, David (2014) 'Latin America Is World's Most Violent Region - WSJ'. *The Wall Street Journal*. [online] Available from: https://www.wsj.com/articles/SB10001424052702303603904579495863883782316 (Accessed 31 January 2023)

98 Partlow, Joshua (2014) 'Kerry Warns of Possible Sanctions Against Venezuela'. *Washington Post*, 21st May.

99 Dayan, Dani (2014) 'Obama Turned Israeli Settlements Into a Deal Breaker - Haaretz Com - Haaretz.com'. *Haaretz*. [online] Available from: https://www.haaretz.com/2014-07-02/ty-article/under-a-cloud/0000017f-db8d-db5a-a57f-dbef8a950000 (Accessed 31 January 2023)

100 Coulter, Ann (2014) 'Gop Crafts Plan To Wreck The Country, Lose Voters - Ann Coulter'. *anncoulter.com*. [online] Available from: https://anncoulter.com/2014/01/29/gop-crafts-plan-to-wreck-the-country-lose-voters/ (Accessed 31 January 2023)

101 Greene, Chad Felix (2014) 'Liberalism's Newest Fake Gay "Victim" - American Thinker'. *American Thinker*. [online] Available from: https://www.americanthinker.com/articles/2014/08/liberalisms_newest_fake_gay_victim.html (Accessed 31 January 2023)

102 Brydum, Sunnivie (2014) 'WATCH: "Christian" Family's Terrifying Response to Son Coming Out'. *Advocate*. [online] Available from: https://www.advocate.com/youth/2014/08/28/watch-christian-familys-terrifying-response-son-coming-out#.VACeYrqthEU.facebook (Accessed 31 January 2023)

103 CNN (2014) 'CNN.com - Transcripts'. *CNN*. [online] Available from: https://transcripts.cnn.com/show/ddhln/date/2014-08-28/segment/01 (Accessed 31 January 2023)

104 BBC (2014) '#BBCtrending: Disowned on video, gay teen speaks out - BBC News'. *BBC*. [online] Available from: https://www.bbc.com/news/blogs-trending-289 77410?ocid=socialflow_twitter (Accessed 31 January 2023)

105 Greene, Chad Felix (2014) 'Christian Faith is Not Hate - American Thinker'. *American Thinker*. [online] Available from: https://www.americanthinker.com/article s/2014/09/christian_faith_is_not_hate.html (Accessed 31 January 2023)

106 Michaelson, Jay (2014) 'The Hateful Pastor All Too Happy to Be Left Behind When It Comes to Gays'. *The Daily Beast*. [online] Available from: https://www.thedailybeast.com/the-hateful-pastor-all-too-happy-to-be-left-behi nd-when-it-comes-to-gays (Accessed 31 January 2023)

107 Edwards, David (2014) 'TN pastor vows not to "repent" for homophobia: God says gays "must be put to death" '. *Rawstory*.

108 Densen, Ryan (2014) '"Christian" Pastor At Mega-Church Calls On Gays To Be "Put To Death" '. *addictinginfo.org*.

109 Greene, Chad Felix (2014) 'A Gay Jew Goes to Church - American Thinker'. *American Thinker*. [online] Available from: https://www.americanthinker.com/article s/2014/09/a_gay_jew_goes_to_church.html (Accessed 31 January 2023)

110 Anon (2010) 'Churches contribute to gay suicides, most Americans believe – CNN Belief Blog - CNN.com Blogs'. *CNN*. [online] Available from: https://religion.blogs.cnn.com/2010/10/21/churches-contribute-to-gay-suicide s-most-americans-believe/ (Accessed 31 January 2023)

111 Brock, Rita Nakashima (2011) 'The Ideological Roots of Christian Terrorism | HuffPost Religion'. *Huffington Post*. [online] Available from: https://www.huffpost.co m/entry/the-ideological-roots-of_b_910023 (Accessed 31 January 2023)

112 Tarico, Valerie (2014) '9 sinister things the Christian right does in the name of God | Salon.com'. *Salon*. [online] Available from: https://www.salon.com/2014/07/18/9_ sinister_things_the_christian_right_does_in_the_name_of_god_partner/ (Accessed 31 January 2023)

113 Goldberg, Michelle (2006) 'What Is Christian Nationalism? | HuffPost Latest News'. *Huffington Post*. [online] Available from: https://www.huffpost.com/entry/wh at-is-christian-nationa_b_20989 (Accessed 31 January 2023)

114 Jamene, Angela (2014) 'The People Christians Are Allowed to Hate | HuffPost Religion'. *Huffington Post*. [online] Available from: https://www.huffpost.com/entry/ the-people-christians-are_b_5157543 (Accessed 31 January 2023)

115 Murray, Micah J. (2013) 'Why I Can't Say "Love the Sinner/Hate the Sin" Anymore | HuffPost Religion'. *Huffington Post*. [online] Available from: https://www.huffpost.com/entry/why-i-cant-say-love-the-sinner-hate-the-sin-anymore_b_4521519 (Accessed 31 January 2023)

116 Greene, Chad Felix (2014) 'Equal Violence, Unequal Justice - American Thinker'. *American Thinker*. [online] Available from: https://www.americanthinker.com/articles/2014/09/equal_violence_unequal_justice.html (Accessed 31 January 2023)

117 Burdo, Alison and Chang, David (2014) 'Persons of Interest in Gay Couple Attack Interviewed by Police – NBC10 Philadelphia'. *NBC Philadelphia*. [online] Available from: https://www.nbcphiladelphia.com/news/national-international/center-city-hate-crime-gay-couple-attacked-social-media-fansince09-photos-suspects/85703/ (Accessed 31 January 2023)

118 Vella, Vinny (2014) '"Hate-crime" victims recount savage Center City beating'. *The Philadelphia Inquirer*. [online] Available from: https://www.inquirer.com/philly/news/breaking/20140916__Hate-crime__victims_recount_savage_Center_City_beating.html?c=r (Accessed 31 January 2023)

119 Anon (2014) 'Gay Couple Attacked By "Intoxicated, Well Dressed" Gang Of Violent Heterosexuals In Philadelphia - Queerty'. *Queerty*. [online] Available from: https://www.queerty.com/gay-couple-attacked-by-intoxicated-well-dressed-gang-of-violent-heterosexuals-in-philadelphia-20140916 (Accessed 31 January 2023)

120 Cesca, Bob (2012) 'Black-on-White Crime and the Reasons for a Media Double-Standard | HuffPost Latest News'. *Huffington Post*. [online] Available from: https://www.huffpost.com/entry/blackonwhite-crime-and-th_b_1521775 (Accessed 31 January 2023)

121 Fiano-Chesser, Cassy (2014) 'Amanda Marcotte: Babies are time-sucking monsters, abortion like removing a cavity - Live Action News'. *LiveAction*. [online] Available from: https://www.liveaction.org/news/amanda-marcotte-babies-are-time-sucking-monsters-abortion-like-removing-a-cavity/ (Accessed 31 January 2023)

122 Anon (2014) 'Obama Weekly Address: Give America A Raise'. *Breitbart*. [online] Available from: https://www.breitbart.com/clips/2014/02/22/obama-weekly-address-give-america-a-raise/ (Accessed 31 January 2023)

123 keepemhonest (2013) 'At this point: the GOP Shutdown is Driven by Pure TeaParty Hate'. *Daily Kos*. [online] Available

from: https://www.dailykos.com/stories/2013/10/03/1243683/-At-this-point-the-G OP-Shutdown-is-Driven-by-Pure-TeaParty-Hate (Accessed 31 January 2023)

124 Tate, Kristin (2014) 'Rep. Sheila Jackson Lee Wants Grants for Jobless'. *Breitbart.* [online] Available from: https://www.breitbart.com/border/2014/02/20/sheila-jackso n-lee-pushing-for/ (Accessed 31 January 2023)

125 Anon (2015) 'Obama to sign executive order raising minimum wage for federal contractors'. *Fox News.* [online] Available from: https://www.foxnews.com/politics/ obama-to-sign-executive-order-raising-minimum-wage-for-federal-contractors (Accessed 31 January 2023)

126 Roy, Avik (2014) 'White House: It's A Good Thing That Obamacare Will Drive 2.5 Million Americans Out Of The Workforce'. *Forbes.* [online] Available from: https://www.forbes.com/sites/theapothecary/2014/02/05/white-house-its-a-good-thin g-that-obamacare-will-drive-2-5-million-americans-out-of-the-workforce/?sh=4230586 42c37 (Accessed 31 January 2023)

127 Johnson, Bridget (2014) 'White House: Employers Can Prevent Job Losses After Minimum Wage Hike by "Accepting Lower Profit Margins" – PJ Media'. *PJMedia.* [online] Available from: https://pjmedia.com/tatler/2014/02/18/white-house-employers-can-prevent-j ob-losses-after-minimum-wage-hike-by-accepting-lower-profit-margins-n188805 (Accessed 31 January 2023)

128 Anon (2013) 'TOP 10 REASONS FOOD STAMPS NEED TO BE REFORMED - FreedomWorks'. *FreedomWorks.* [online] Available from: https://www.f reedomworks.org/top-10-reasons-food-stamps-need-to-be-reformed/ (Accessed 31 January 2023)

129 Bluey, Rob (2012) 'Chart of the Week: Nearly Half of All Americans Don't Pay Income Taxes'. *The Daily Signal.* [online] Available from: https://www.dailysignal.com//2012/02/19/chart-of-the-week-nearly-half-of-all -americans-dont-pay-income-taxes/ (Accessed 31 January 2023)